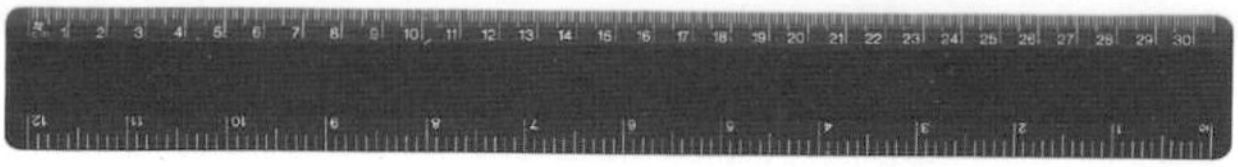

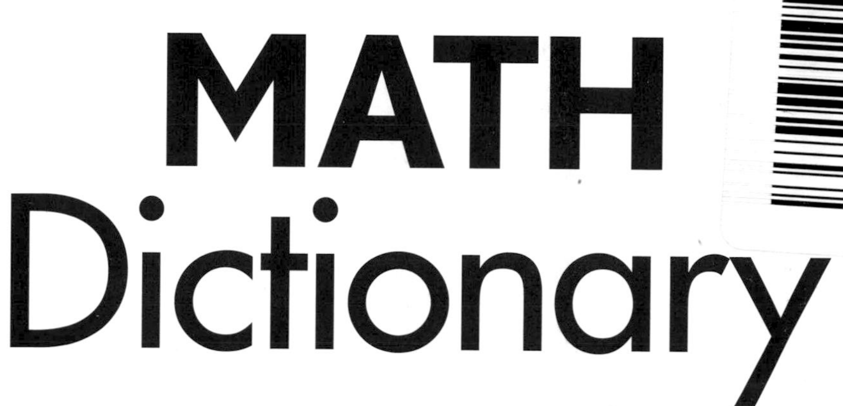

MATH Dictionary

Canadian Edition

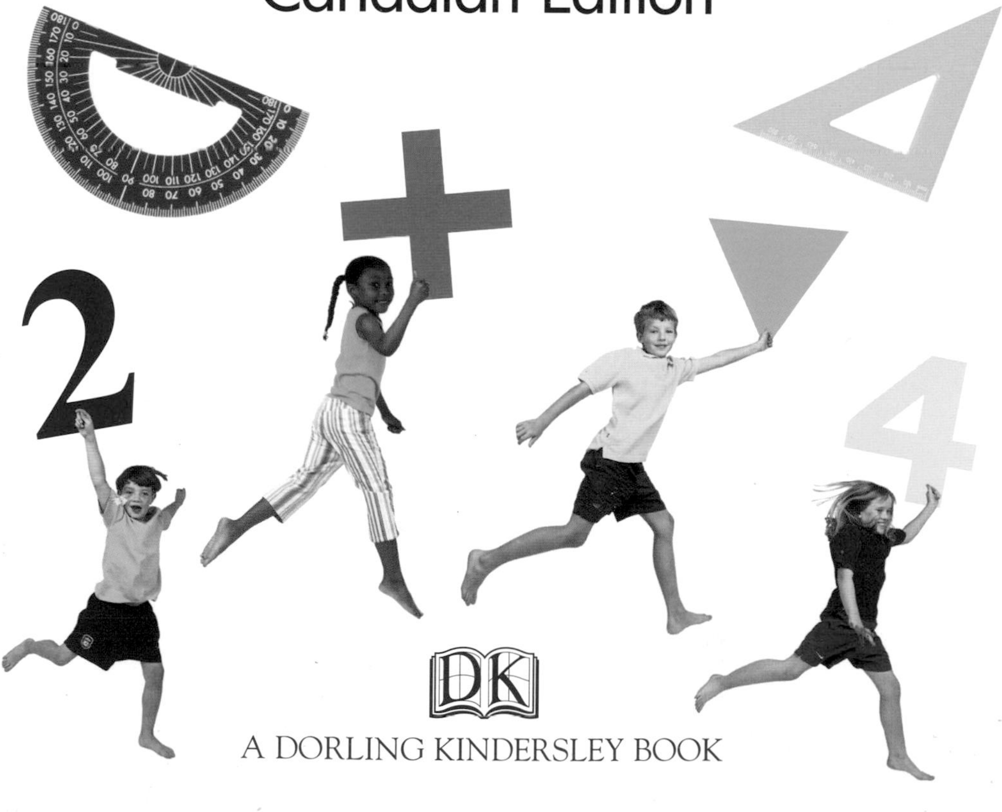

DK
A DORLING KINDERSLEY BOOK

Author Judith de Klerk
Designed and edited by Tall Tree Ltd
Additional editing by Lee Wilson, Penny Smith, Fleur Star, Carrie Love, Caroline Stamps
Additional design by Hedi Hunter, Lauren Rosier
Art director Rachael Foster
Publishing manager Bridget Giles
Production editor Siu Yin Chan
Production controller Claire Pearson
Jacket designer Natalie Godwin
Jacket editor Mariza O'Keeffe
Canadian editor Barbara Campbell
Math consultants Sean McArdle, Marilyn Wilson

First Canadian Edition, 2009
This paperback edition published in 2011
Dorling Kindersley is represented in Canada by
Tourmaline Editions Inc., 662 King Street West, Suite 304
Toronto, Ontario M5V 1M7

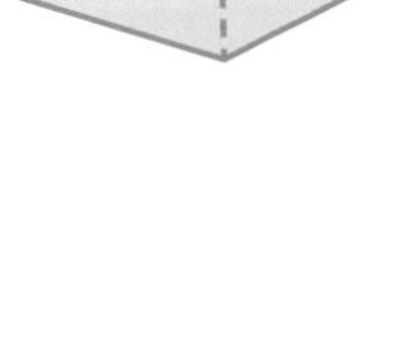

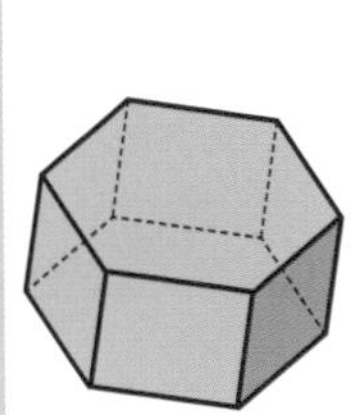

10 9 8 7 6 5 4 3 2 1
014 – MD584 – Aug/11

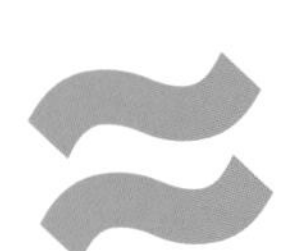

Published in Great Britain by Dorling Kindersley Limited

Library and Archives Canada Cataloguing in Publication
Vorderman, Carol
Math dictionary / Carol Vorderman. -- Canadian ed.
Hardcover ISBN 978-1-55363-106-4
Paperback ISBN 978-1-55363-110-1
1. Mathematics--Dictionaries, Juvenile. I. Title.
QA5.V67 2009 j510.3 C2008-907462-9

Color reproduction by Media Development Printing Ltd, UK
Printed and bound by Leo, China

Discover more at
www.dk.com

Contents

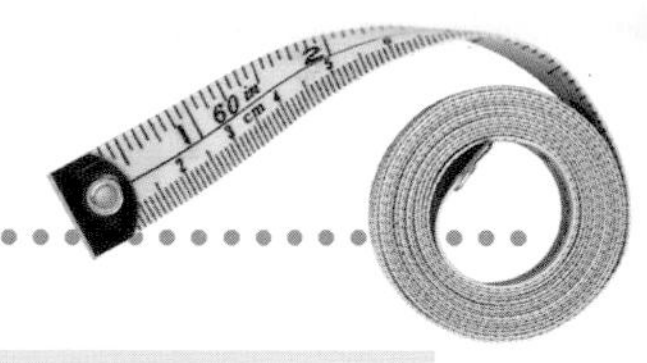

Introduction

Math Dictionary contains everything you need to know to get ahead in primary school math. Whether you're stuck on symbols or need a hand with homework, the dictionary is here to help.

Inside this dictionary you'll find:

A–Z pages Simple, clear definitions of hundreds of mathematical terms. Photographs, illustrations, and diagrams help explain each term, while working examples show how the term is used in practice. Cross-references to entries on related subjects give extra information.

Fast search index It's quick and easy to find your way around the dictionary using the highlighted words and coloured index bars.

Quick reference section Turn to these handy tables to look up symbols, useful number words, prefixes, units of measurement, and how to convert metric and imperial measures.

How to use the A–Z pages

Main entries are in large, bold type.

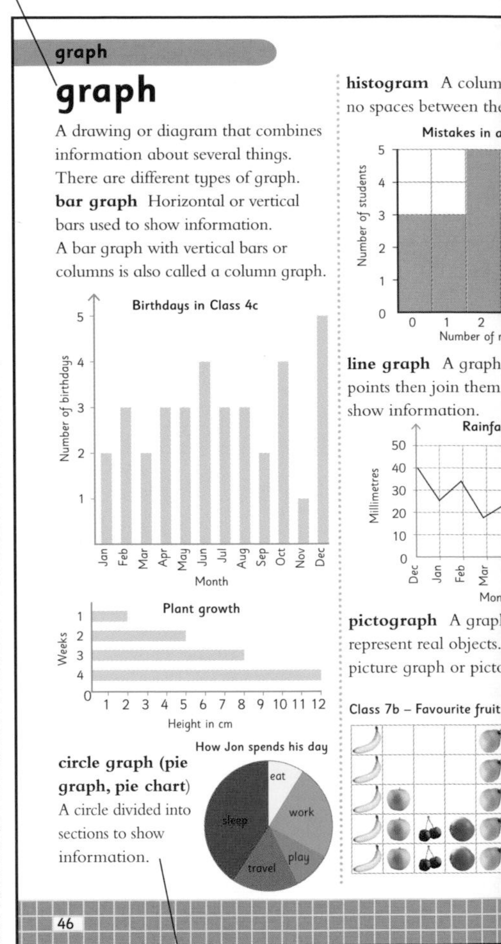

Sub-entries of related words are in smaller bold type.

hundreds of entries from abacus to zero

easy-to-read layout

coloured panels of expanded entries link related words together

Find out symbols and similar terms at a glance.

Working examples help you to understand how the term is used.

graph paper
See **square paper**

greater than
Symbol >
More than, bigger than.
An expression that shows which number is larger in a pair of numbers.

7 > 6
7 is greater than 6

See **inequality, less than**

grid
Sets of parallel lines that cross each other at right angles. Grids are often found on maps and graphs.

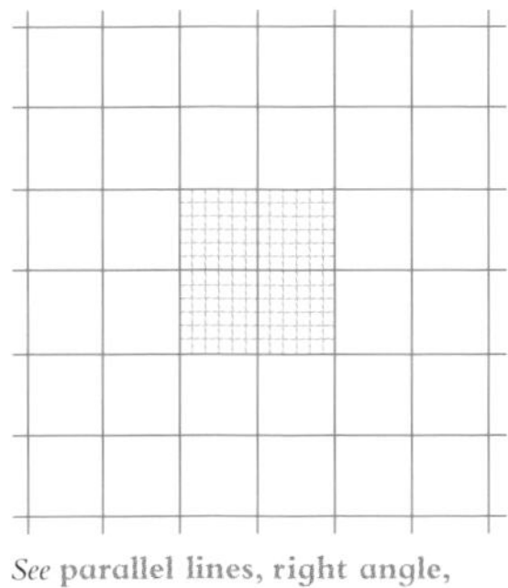

See **parallel lines, right angle, square paper**

gross
Twelve dozen (12 × 12); 144.

group
1. Putting things together in a set or group. In the decimal system, things are grouped into tens.

hundreds	tens	units
2	4	3

243 = 2 groups of 100
4 groups of 10
3 groups of 1

2. Two or more things.

a group of boys

grouping Putting things together into sets with the same number in each set. This is also called quotition.

How many groups of four can be made with twenty balls?

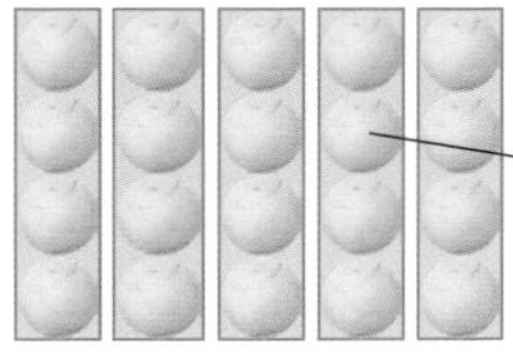

The answer is five groups of four.
See **division, set**

a b c d e f g h i j k l m n o p q r s t u v w x y z

47

quick reference tables at the back of the book

Find what you're looking for quickly and easily.

accessible

Photographs, illustrations, and diagrams help explain the term.

ideal homework help

Follow these links to find words with related meanings.

user friendly

abacus

A counting frame with beads that slide up and down rods. An abacus is used for counting and calculating.

absolute value

Symbol | |

How far a number is from 0 on a number line, on either side of 0. The absolute value of a number is never negative.

Example

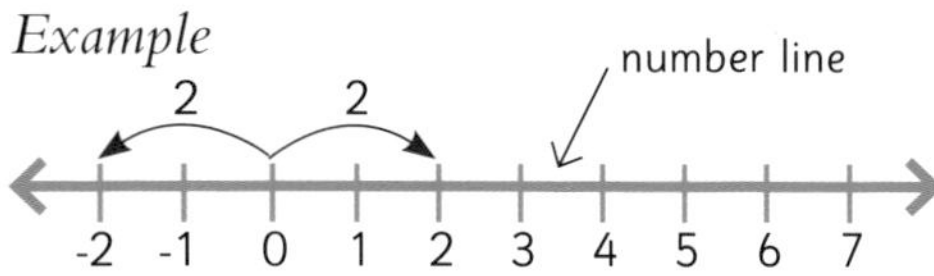

The absolute value of -2 and 2 is 2.

accurate

Exact, correct, without a mistake.

See **approximation**

acute

Sharp, sharply pointed.

acute angle A sharply pointed angle that is less than a right angle.

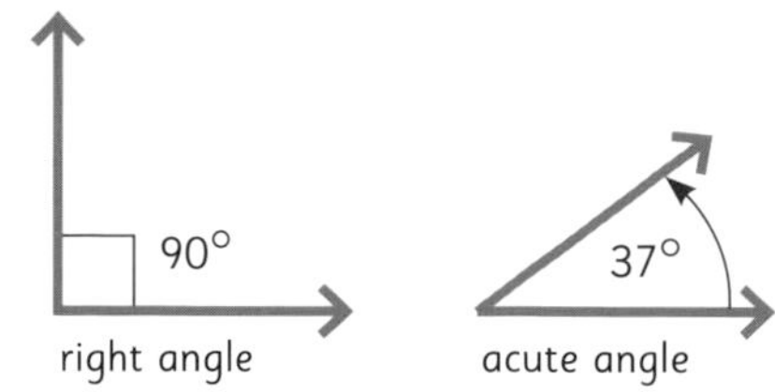

acute triangle
A triangle that has three acute inside angles.

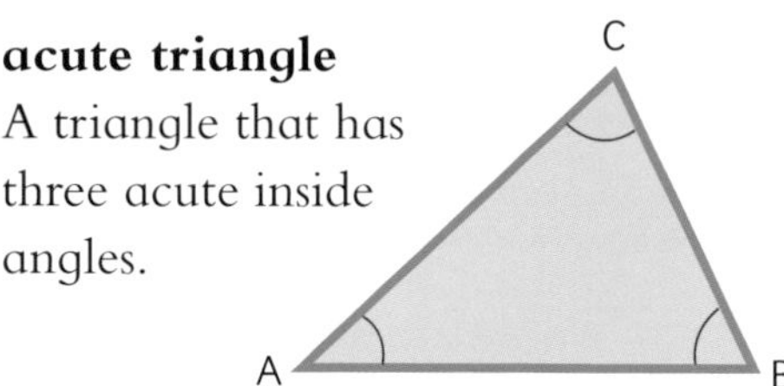

See **angle, triangle**

addition

add, adding

Symbol +

Joining two or more numbers together to make a larger number.

2 + 3 = 5

20 + 30 = 50

200 + 300 = 500

+ =

2 3

-2 -1 0 1 2 3 4 5 6 7

This number line shows 2 + 3 = 5.

addend The number being added.

2 + 6 = 8

addend ↑ ↑ addend

additive inverse When we add a number and its inverse (opposite), the answer is always zero.

8 + −8 = 0

number ↑ ↑ inverse

repeated addition Adding the same number to itself a number of times.

3 + 3 + 3 + 3 = 12

column addition Placing addends in columns, so that the units, tens, etc are lined up.

43	57	24
21	15	72
64	72	96

tens ↑ ↑ units

See **inverse, number line, sum, zero**

adjacent

Next to each other, having a common point or side.

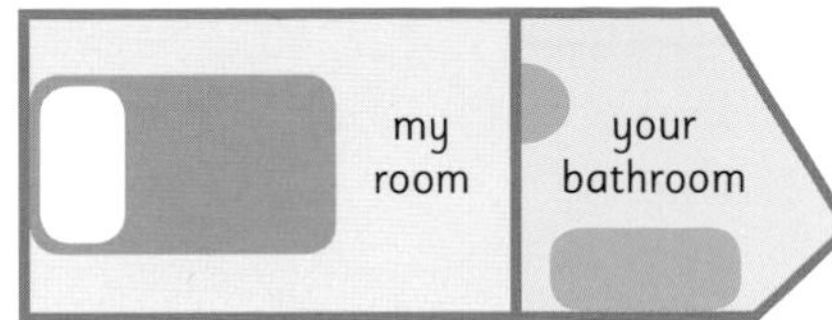

My room is adjacent to your bathroom.

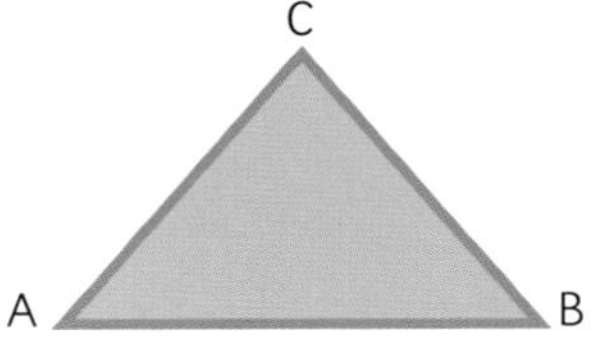

Side AB is adjacent to side AC.

algebra

An area of mathematics that uses letters and symbols to represent numbers and quantities.

flower + *flower* = *2 flowers*

5 − x = 2

algebraic expression A calculation that contains at least one number and one unknown number (variable), but no equals sign.

3y − x

verbal expression Using words to explain an algebraic expression.

algorithm

A set of rules or a method that you use to solve a problem.

Example Use blocks to find how many 3 × 4 is.

Step 1: Lay down one lot of four blocks.

Step 2: Now put down the second and third lots of four.

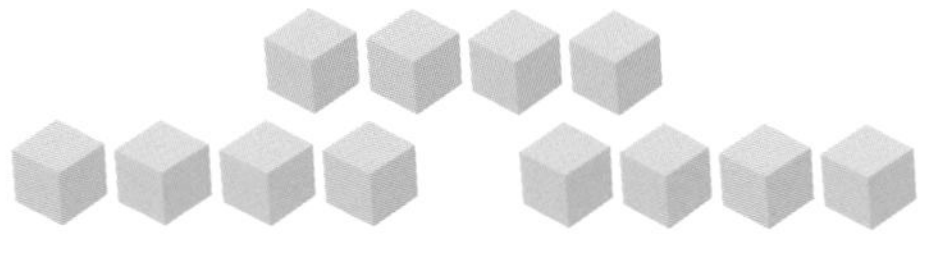

Step 3: Exchange 10 units for one ten (long).

Step 4: Write down your answer.
3 × 4 = 12

See **base ten blocks**

align

Lay or place in a straight line.

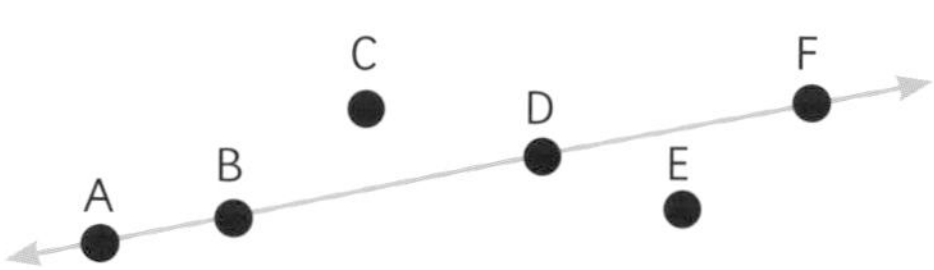

A, B, D, and F are aligned, but C and E are not.

See **line**

altitude

Height. How high something is above the surface of the Earth or sea.

The altitude of this airplane is 2000 metres.

See **height**

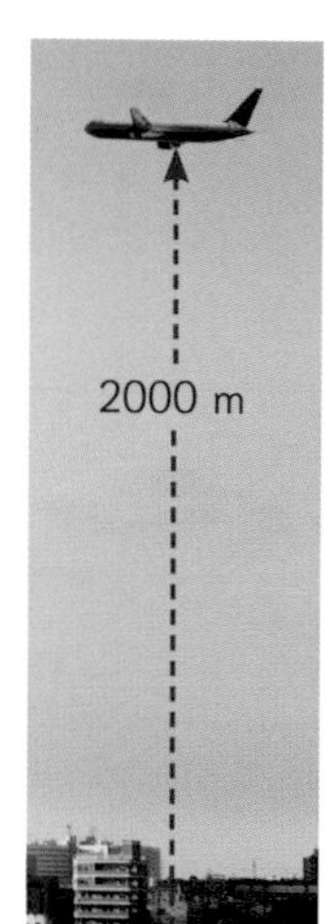

a.m. (ante meridiem)

See **time**

angle

The amount of turn about a fixed point (vertex). Angles are measured in degrees (°).

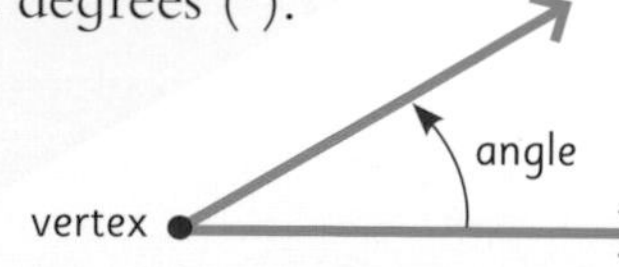

alternate angles The two equal but opposite angles on a "Z" shape.

angle name Letters are often used to represent angles.

angle sum The angles in a polygon (flat shape) added together. The angle sum of any triangle is 180°.

a° + b° + c° = 180°

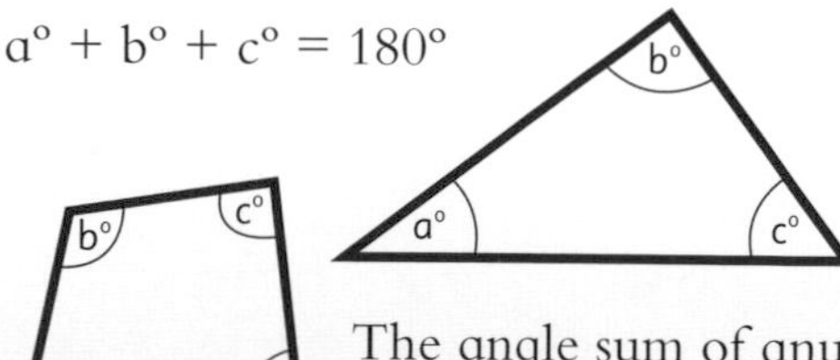

The angle sum of any quadrilateral is 360°.

a° + b° + c° + d° = 360°

amount

The total of a number of things or how much you have of a thing.
Example This is the amount of money in my purse.

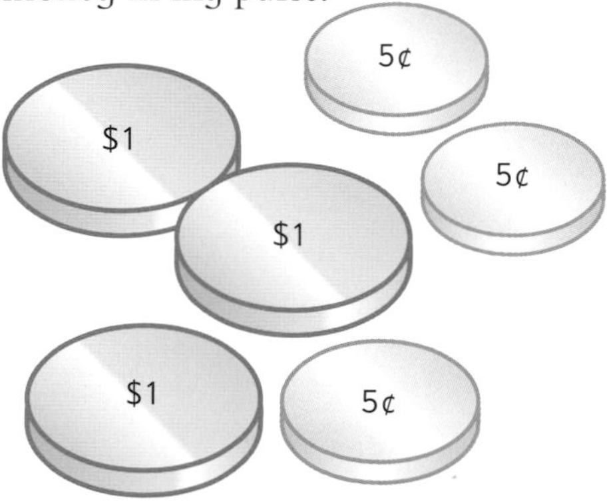

analogue clock

A clock or watch with the numbers 1 to 12 written on its face, and two hands pointing at them to show the time.
See **digital clock**

annual

1. Happening only once a year.
Example Annual flower show.
2. Recurring yearly.
Example The annual rate of interest is 6%.
See **interest, percent**

per annum (p.a.) A term that means "each year".

anticlockwise

Turning the opposite way to the hands of a clock. Screws and bottle tops are loosened anticlockwise. The term "counterclockwise" is used in North America.

Example
If a clock is ten minutes fast, the hands must be moved anticlockwise ten minutes.
See **clockwise, counterclockwise**

arm of an angle
One of the lines that makes an angle.

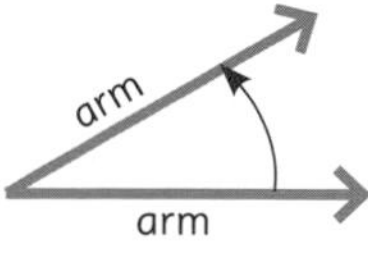

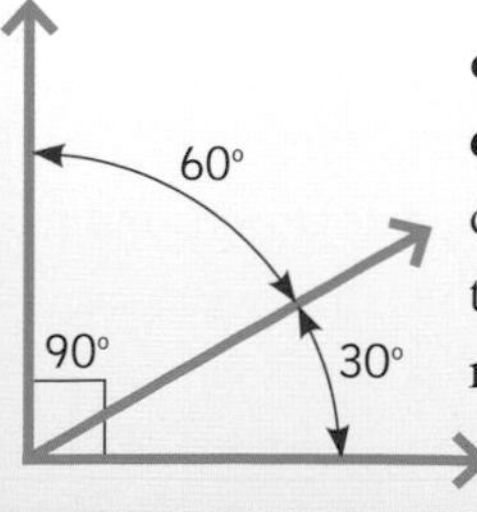

complementary angles Two angles that together measure 90°.

corresponding angles Equal angles created when two parallel lines are crossed by a straight line.

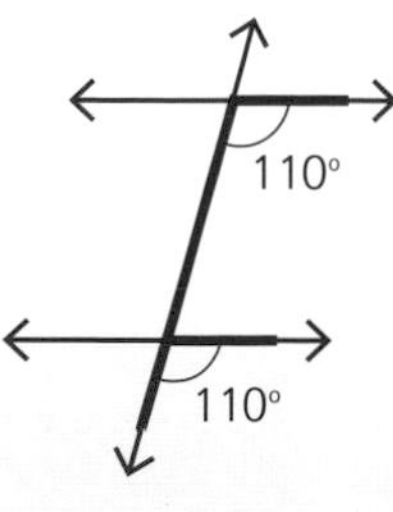

See **acute, degree, obtuse angle, parallel lines, reflex angle, right angle, straight angle, vertex**

a b c d e f g h i j k l m n o p q r s t u v w x y z

apex

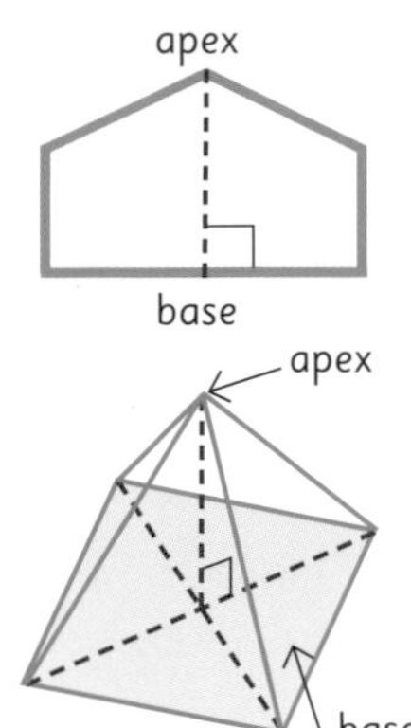

Plural apexes
The top; the highest point; the point furthest from the base. Also called the vertex.
See **base, vertex**

approximation

approximating, approximately
Symbols ≈ ≑ ≏
A result that is nearly but not exactly the answer.
One way to approximate is to calculate an answer by rounding the numbers up or down.
Example
$0.9 \approx 1$
$798 \times 2.1 \approx 800 \times 2 \approx 1600$
See **accurate, rounding**

arbitrary unit

Something we use to help us measure. Handspan, pace, and objects such as counters, bottle tops, and apples are all arbitrary units.

Example The area of this rectangle is 16 apples.

See **handspan, pace**

arc

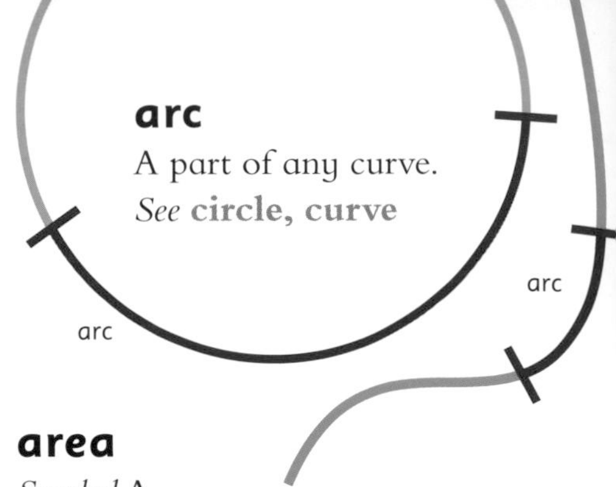

A part of any curve.
See **circle, curve**

area

Symbol A
The size of, or amount of a surface. Area is measured in square units such as square centimetres (cm^2).

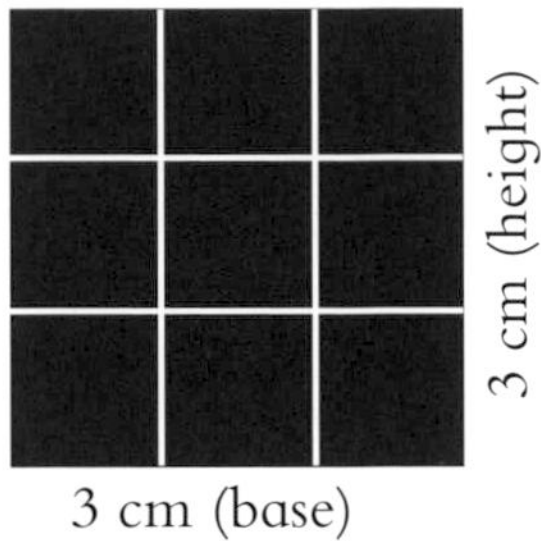

3 cm (base) × 3 cm (height) = 9 cm^2
See **conservation of area, formula, surface, unit of measurement**

arithmetic

The part of mathematics that deals with numbers. We use arithmetic for calculations with decimals, whole numbers, and fractions.
This includes addition, subtraction, multiplication, and division.
Arithmetic is also used for measuring, solving word problems, and working with money.
See **computation**

array

Arrangement of objects or numbers in columns or rows.

an array of sheep

arrow diagram

A diagram that uses arrows to show a connection between two things.

Examples

1. The connection between a set of numbers.

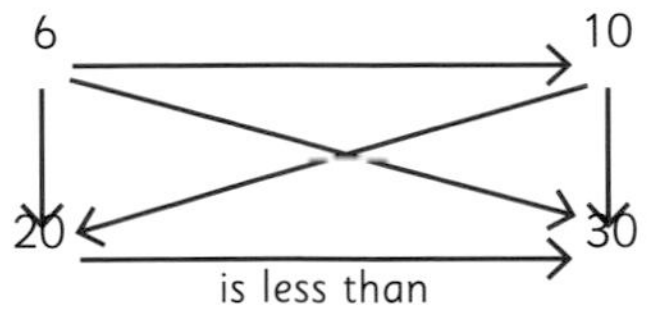

2. The connection, or relationship between two sets.

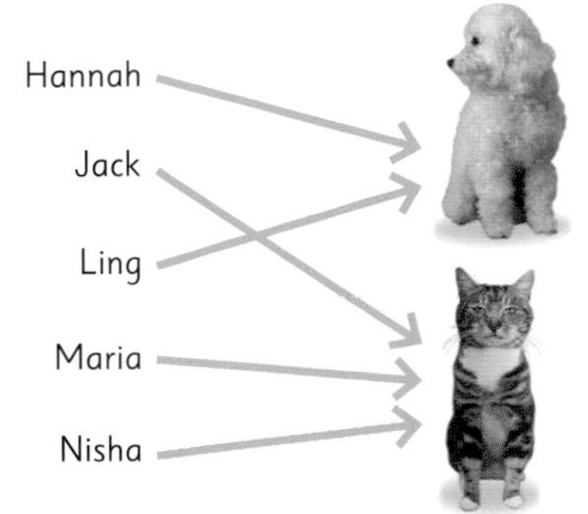

Children and their favourite pets

many-to-one correspondence

This is when several items in the first set are associated with one item in the second set.

See **mapping, one-to-one correspondence, relation, set**

ascending order

Going upwards or increasing in value.

See **increase, order, pattern, sequence**

askew

Not straight; at an angle.

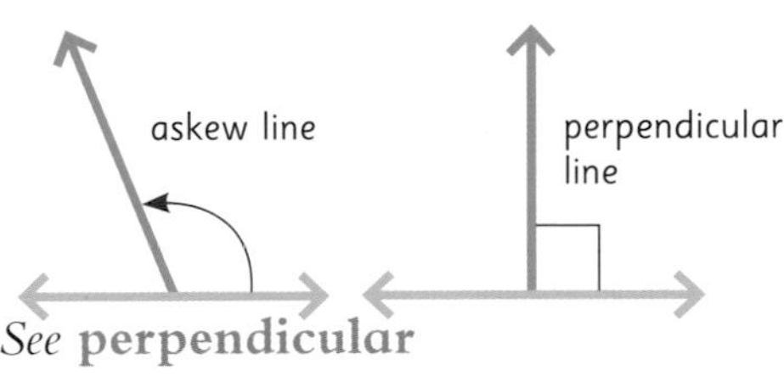

See **perpendicular**

associative property

The associative properties of addition and multiplication say that when you add or multiply three or more numbers together, it doesn't matter how you group them, the answer is the same.

Examples

Addition: $3 + 7 + 9 = 19$

so $3 + 7 = 10; 10 + 9 = 19$

or $7 + 9 = 16; 16 + 3 = 19$

Multiplication: $3 \times 7 \times 9 = 189$

so $3 \times 7 = 21; 21 \times 9 = 189$

or $7 \times 9 = 63; 63 \times 3 = 189$

See **commutative property**

asymmetry

Having parts that are not equal (symmetrical) in some way. An object that has no line of symmetry is described as asymmetrical.

See **line of symmetry, symmetry**

attribute

A characteristic of an object, such as size, shape, or colour.
See **classification, property**

average

One single number that represents a middle value in a set of numbers. It is found by adding all the numbers and dividing the answer (sum) by the number of those numbers.

Example Find the average of numbers 2, 5, 4, 6, and 3.

$$\text{average} = \frac{\text{sum of numbers}}{\text{number of those numbers}}$$

$$= \frac{2 + 5 + 4 + 6 + 3}{5}$$

$$= \frac{20}{5}$$

$$\text{average} = 4$$

This is also called the mean or arithmetic mean.
See **mean, medium, mode**

axis

Plural axes

1. The lines that make a graph's framework.

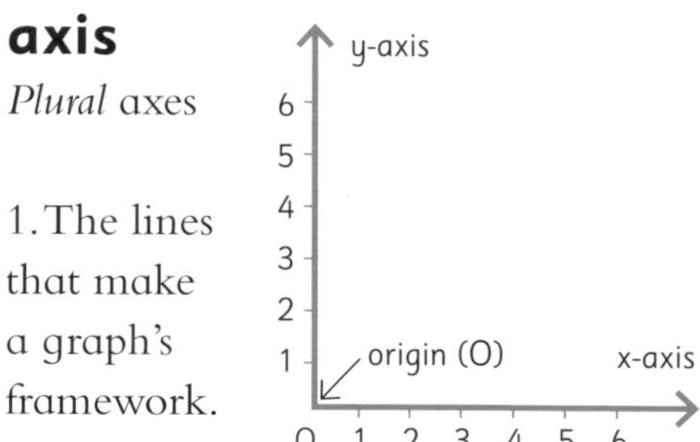

2. A line going through the centre of a figure or solid. When the parts on either side of the axis look the same, it is also called an axis of symmetry.

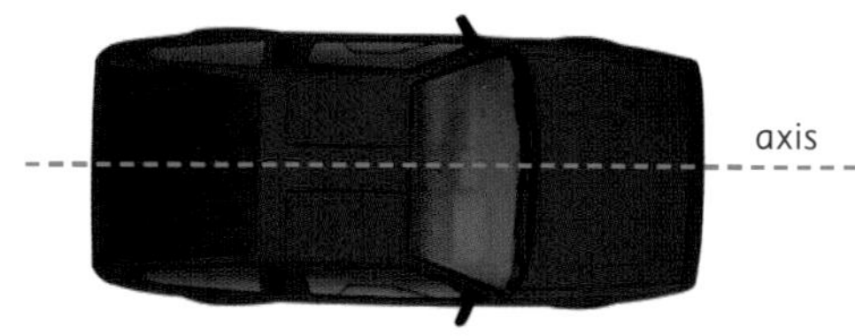

See **coordinates, graph, line of symmetry, origin**

Bb

balance

1. An equal distribution of weight.

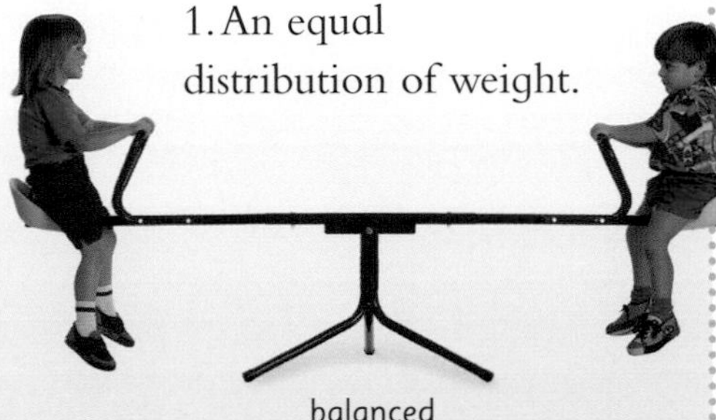

balanced

unbalanced

2. Balance scales are a kind of scale used to weigh things.

3. The amount of money in a bank account.

You have a bank account containing.....$50.00

You take out ....$10.00 to buy a toy

Your balance is now....$40.00

bar graph

See **graph**

base

The face (surface) on which a shape or a solid stands.

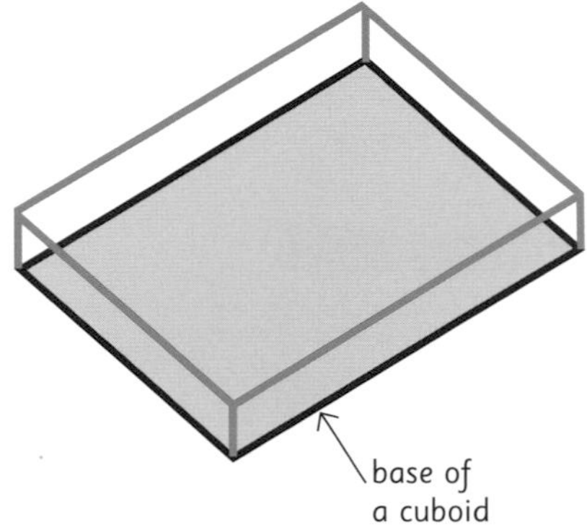

base line

1. The horizontal axis of a graph is sometimes called the base line.

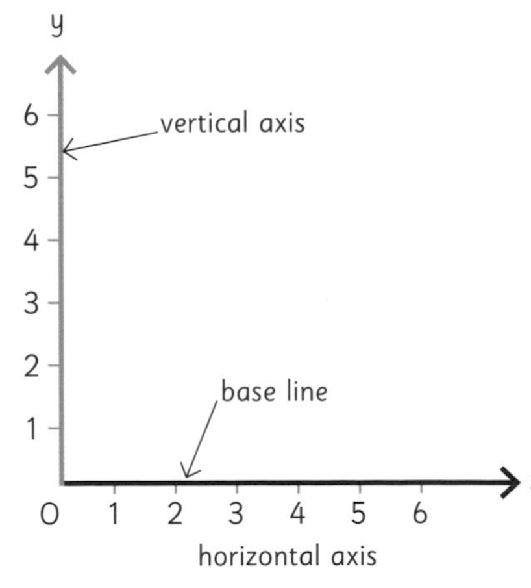

2. A base from which the heights of objects may be compared.

See **axis, horizontal line, vertical**

base ten blocks

A set of wooden or plastic blocks used to represent a number. The most commonly used are the base ten blocks.

A set of base ten blocks consists of:

small cubes – units or ones

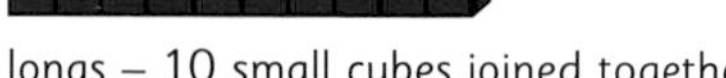
longs – 10 small cubes joined together

squares – 100 small cubes formed into a square

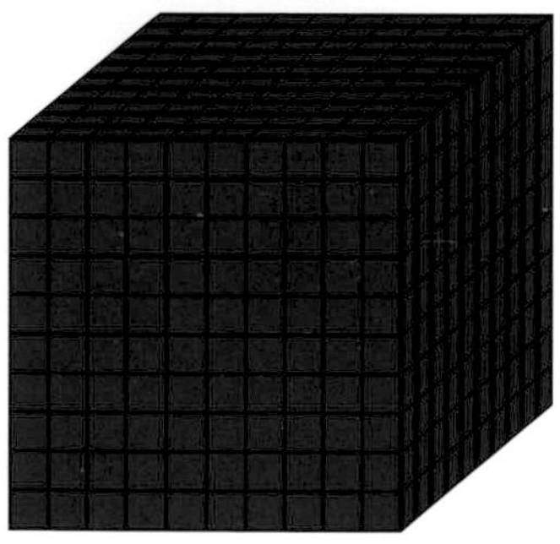
large cubes – 1000 small cubes formed into a large cube

base ten system

The number system we use every day. We use 10 digits (0, 1, 2, 3, 4, 5, 6, 7, 8, 9) to make all our numbers.
See **decimal place-value system**

basic facts

Operations (adding, subtracting, multiplying, and dividing) performed with one digit numbers 0, 1, 2, 3, 4, 5, 6, 7, 8, and 9.

Addition

$0 + 0 = 0 \quad 0 + 1 = 1$

$1 + 1 = 2 \quad 9 + 9 = 18$

Multiplication

$0 \times 0 = 0 \quad 0 \times 1 = 0$

$1 \times 1 = 1 \quad 9 \times 9 = 81$

See **digit, operation, zero**

beam balance

Any balance where a beam is used.

A beam balance is used to measure the mass of an object. It does this by balancing it with an object whose mass is known.
See **balance, mass**

bi

A prefix added to the front of words and meaning two or twice.

Examples

bicentenary

The 200th anniversary of an event.

A **bi**cycle has two wheels.

See **bisect**

billion

In English-speaking countries, a billion means a thousand millions. It is written like this:

1 000 000 000

In much of the world, a billion means a million millions, and is written:

1 000 000 000 000

binary

A base-2 number system that uses only two digits (0 and 1) to represent numbers. All numbers can be represented in a binary system. Computer systems are often written using binary codes.

bisector

A line that divides a segment, a line or a figure into two equal halves.

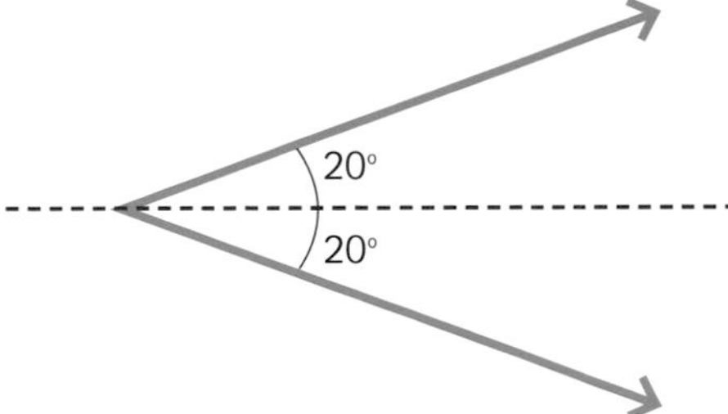

This angle has been bisected.

boundary

A line around the edge of a region. The boundary of this hexagon is its perimeter.

See **perimeter, region**

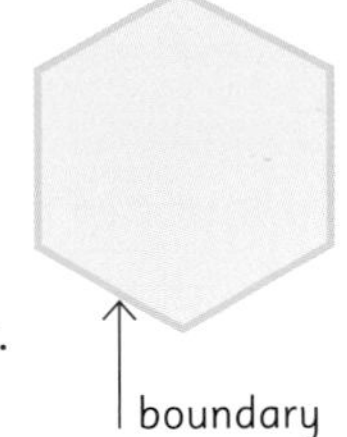

brackets

The signs ( ) [ ] { } are used for grouping things or numbers together. In a calculation, you work out the numbers in the brackets first.

$$25 - (2 + 3) = ?$$
$$2 + 3 = 5$$
$$25 - 5 = 20$$

See **order of operations**

breadth

Another word for "width", the measurement of something from one side to the opposite side.

See **width**

a b c d e f g h i j k l m n o p q r s t u v w x y z

Cc

calculate

To work out the answer.

calorie

Symbol kcal, cal

A term for measuring the energy of food, also known as kilocalorie. It is the amount of energy needed to heat 1 kg of water by 1°C. A medium-sized (160 g) orange contains 59 kcal.

cancelling

Changing a fraction to its simplest form. The value of the fraction stays the same, but having smaller numbers makes it easier to work with.

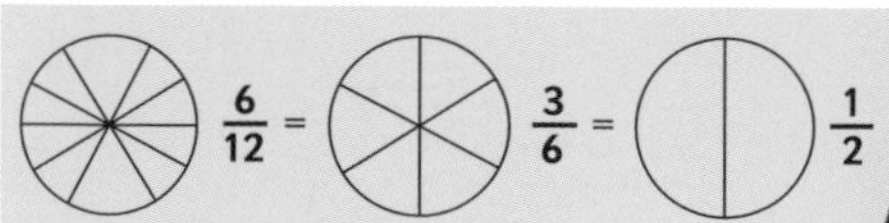

Cancelling is done by dividing the numerator and denominator by the same number.

numerator / denominator

$$\frac{15 \div 3}{21 \div 3} = \frac{\cancel{15}\,5}{\cancel{21}\,7} = \frac{5}{7}$$

See **denominator, factors, fraction, numerator**

capacity

The amount a container can hold. Capacity is measured in cubic units, such as cubic centimetres (cm^3).

The capacity of the big carton of milk is 1000 cm^3.

The amount (volume) of milk in a full carton is 1 litre.

The capacity of the carton will stay the same even when some of the milk is poured out.

MILK 1 litre

MILK $\frac{1}{2}$ litre

See **cubic unit, volume**

cardinal number

The number of all elements (items) in a set. When we count, we give each element a number, starting with 1. These numbers are in sequence. The last number given is the set's cardinal number.

1 2 3 4

Example

How many balloons?

The cardinal number of this set of balloons is 4.

See **counting, sequence, set**

Carroll diagram

See **diagram**

carrying

In arithmetic, taking a number over to the next column when the numbers in one column come to more than nine.

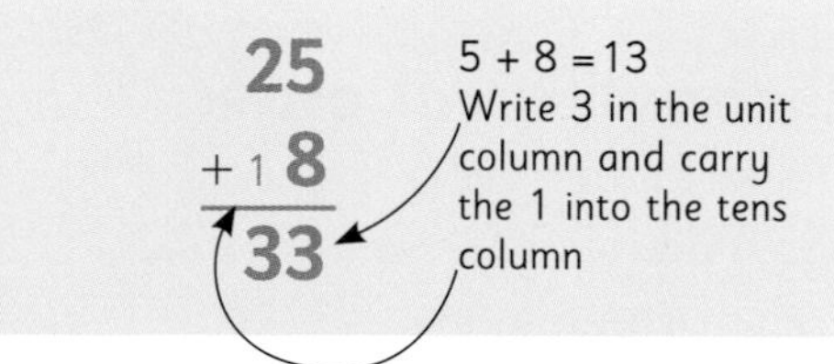

Celsius

Symbol °C

A scale used for measuring temperature. Water freezes at 0°C and boils at 100°C. Celsius is also known as centigrade.

Water boils at 100°C.

See **temperature, thermometer**

cent

Symbol ¢

A unit of money in some countries. One cent is one hundredth of a dollar.

1¢ = $0.01 $1 = 100¢

See **dollar**

centi

A prefix meaning one hundredth. One centimetre is one hundredth of a metre.

1 cm = 0.01 m

centigram

Symbol cg

A metric unit of mass.

100 cg = 1gram

Each small line on this scale represents 1 cg.

centimetre *Symbol* cm. A metric unit of length. 100 cm = 1 metre

See **capacity, decimal, length, unit of measurement**

centre

A point in the middle of something that is the same distance from all outer points.

See **circle, radius**

century

One hundred.

100 years

From 1 January 1901 to 31 December 2000 is the 20th century. The 21st century began on 1 January 2001.

a b c d e f g h i j k l m n o p q r s t u v w x y z

certain
A 100% chance of an event happening.
See **chance, event, probability**

chance
A likelihood of an event happening.
See **event, probability**

checking
A way of making sure that an answer is correct. One way of checking is by using an inverse (opposite) calculation.

1. Addition is checked by subtraction.

15 + 28 = 43
43 – 28 = 15

The answer 43 is correct.

2. Division is checked by multiplication.

20 ÷ 4 = 5
5 × 4 = 20

The answer 5 is correct.
See **inverse**

chronological order
The arrangement of events by when they happened, with the earliest coming first.

09:00 a.m.	Homeroom
09:30 a.m.	English
11:00 a.m.	Math
12:30 a.m.	Lunch

The timetable is in chronological order.
See **time**

circle
A 2-D shape that has a curved edge, with each part of the curve the same distance away from the shape's centre.

chord A line that joins two points on a circle's edge. The diameter is the longest chord in a circle, and always goes through the circle's centre.

circle graph Another name for a pie graph.

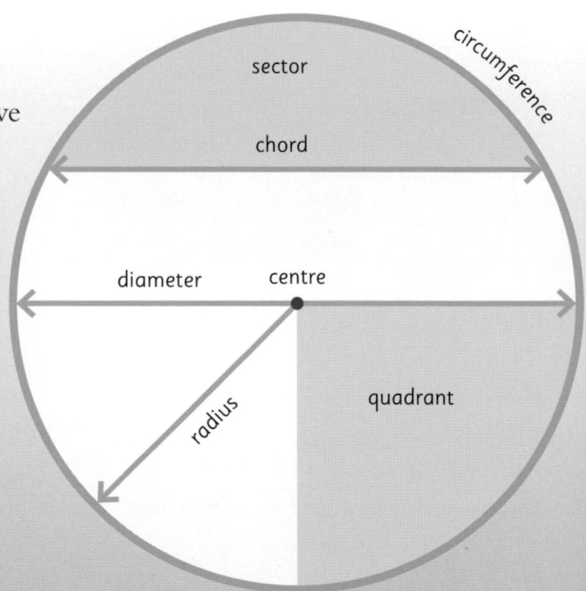

circle

A round 2-D shape (see box below).

class

A group, set, or collection of things. Triangles, squares, rectangles, and kites belong to the class of polygons.

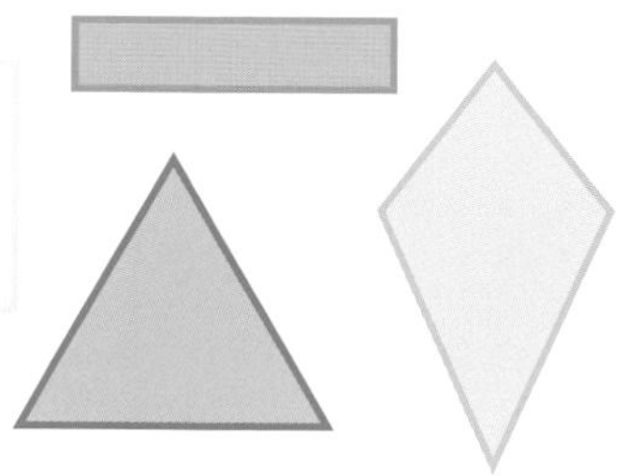

classification

Organization into classes, sets, or groups, according to attributes.

See **attribute, property, sorting**

clockwise

The direction in which the hands of a clock normally travel. Screws and bottle tops are tightened clockwise.

A clock's hands move in a clockwise direction.

See **anticlockwise, counterclockwise**

circular In the form of a circle; round. Something in the form of half a circle is semi-circular.

A protractor is semi-circular.

circumference The edge, or perimeter, of a circle. The distance around a circle.

See **centre, diameter, graph, perimeter, pi, plane, quadrant, radius, sector**

A dart board is circular.

closed figure

A 2-D figure (polygon) with sides that begin and end at the same point.
See **polygon, shape**

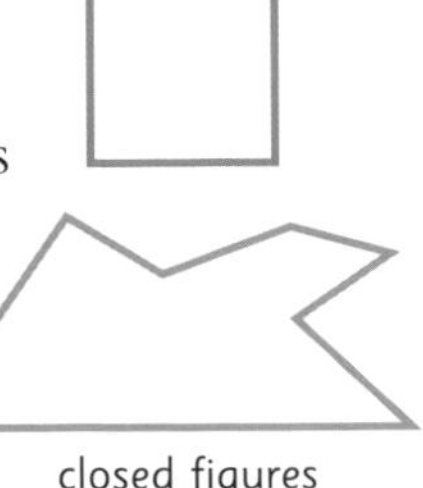

closed figures

code

A system of words, letters, or symbols that represents other letters, words, or sentences. Codes are used for secret writing or signalling.

/—— /——— /— /•••• /• /•—• /
(M O T H E R)

This is "mother" in Morse code.

coefficient

The number in front of a variable in an algebraic term.

3y 3 is the coefficient of y.
See **algebra, variable**

column

A vertical arrangement.

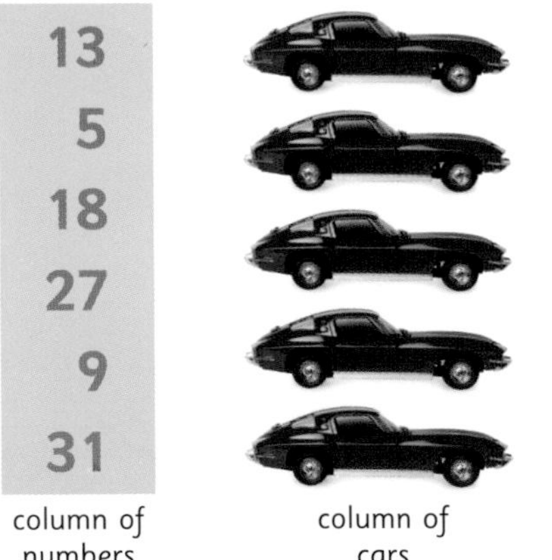

column of numbers

column of cars

combination

A way of grouping objects together. There are four shapes in this group:

Possible pairings include:

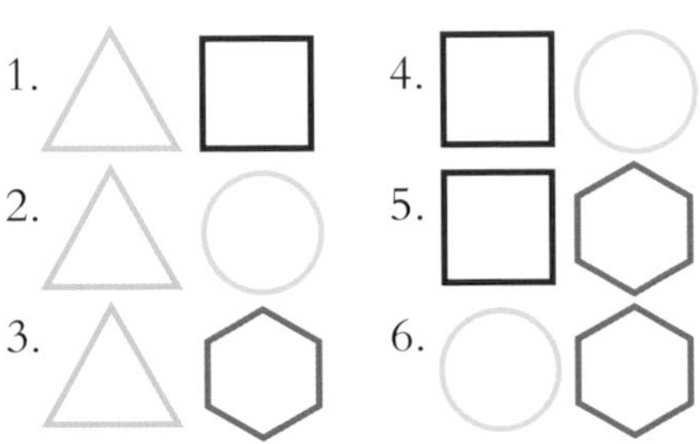

Each pairing is a combination. The order in which the shapes are placed is not important.
See **permutation, set, subset**

combined shapes

2-D shapes that are made of two or more polygons. They are also known as complex shapes.

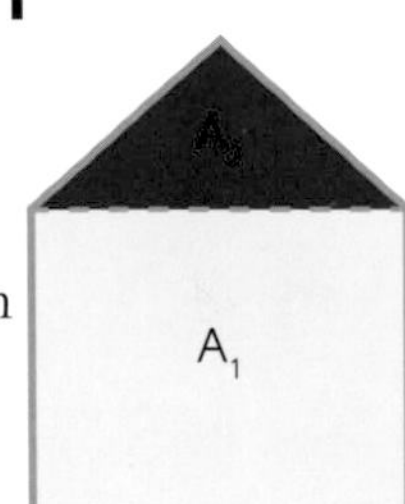

To calculate the area of a combined shape:

1. First divide it into simple shapes.
2. Find the area of each shape.
3. Add the areas to find the total.

$A_1 + A_2 =$ Total area

See **area**

common denominator

A number that all the denominators for two or more fractions divide into exactly.

$\frac{1}{2}$ $\frac{1}{3}$

denominator

These denominators divide exactly into 6, 12, and 18, so 6, 12, and 18 are their common denominators.

See **denominator, fraction, lowest common denominator**

common fraction

See **fraction**

commutative property

We can add or multiply two or more numbers in any order and the answer will be the same.

$6 + 4 = 10$
$4 + 6 = 10$

$3 \times 8 = 24$
$8 \times 3 = 24$

See **associative property**

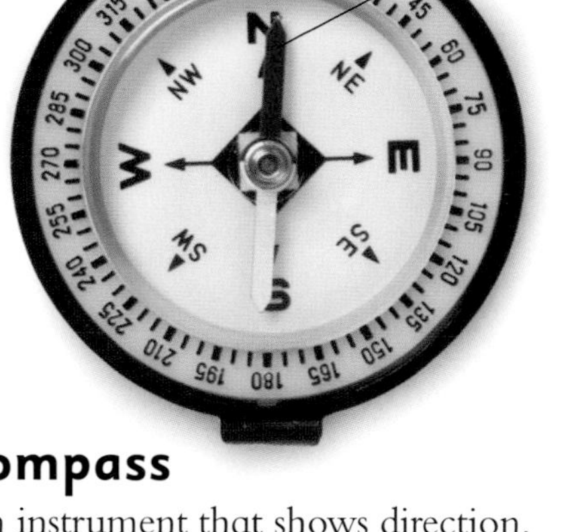

compass

An instrument that shows direction. It is marked with the directions north (N), east (E), south (S), and west (W). The compass needle always points northwards. All other directions can be found by lining up the needle with N.

compass bearing The direction of something in relation to north. It is usually measured in degrees.

comparison

Looking at objects, measures, or quantities to see how they are the same and how they are different.

See **division, ratio**

same heights

different heights

compasses

An instrument that is designed for drawing a circle and marking off equal lengths. Also known as a pair of compasses.

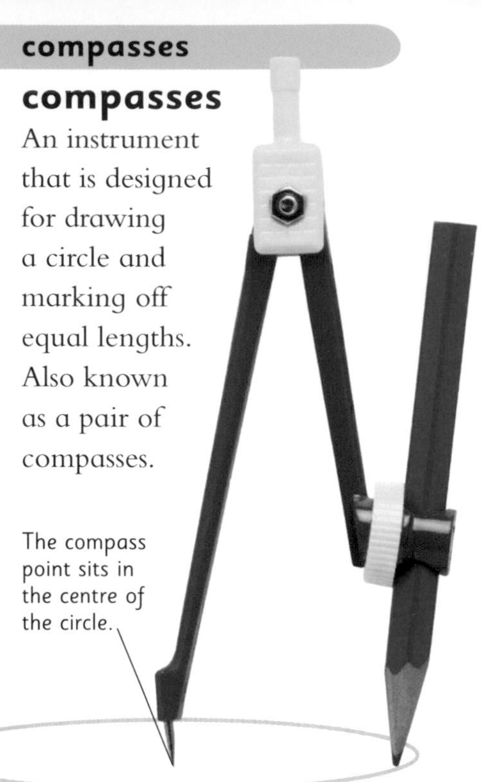

compatible numbers

Numbers that make it easier to estimate the answer to multiplication or division sums because they are easy to multiply or divide.
Example To estimate 42×9, 42 is rounded down to 40 and 9 is rounded up to 10. $40 \times 10 = 400$. 40 and 10 are compatible numbers.
See **estimate, rounding**

complement

Something that completes or fills up a whole.
Example
20 and 80 are complements of 100.

complementary addition

1. Finding the amount needed to complete a set. *Example* What has to be added to 7 to make 10?

7 + ? = 10

Three has to be added.

2. Counting on to a higher total.
Example
My shopping costs $17.50.
I pay with a $20 bill.
How much change should I get?
My change is worked out by counting on to find out what must be added to $17.50 to get $20.
I get $2.50 change.

$17.50 + ? = $20

3. The method of "subtracting" that changes the subtraction question to an addition question.
Example

? – 19 = 2

could be viewed as:

19 + 2 = ?

The answer is 21.
See **addition, subtraction**

composite number

A number with factors other than itself and 1. Factors are whole numbers that divide exactly into another number.

$12 = 12 \times 1$

or 3×4

or 6×2

or $3 \times 2 \times 2$

Twelve is a composite number. Every whole number greater than 1 is either a composite number (4, 6, 8, 9, 10, 12, 14…), or a prime number (2, 3, 5, 7, 11…).

See **factors, prime number**

computation

compute, computing

Using addition, subtraction, multiplication, or division to calculate (work out) the answer to a mathematical question. These operations can be done mentally, in writing, or with the help of calculating aids such as an abacus, tables, calculators, or computers.

See **abacus, operation, table**

concave

A shape that is rounded inwards or hollowed like the inside of a bowl.

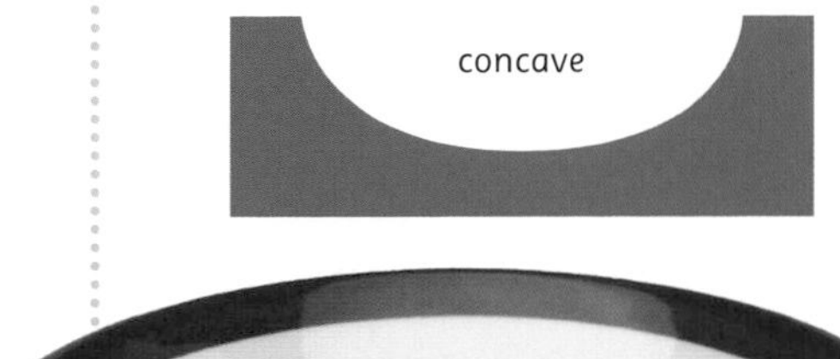

See **convex**

concentric circles

Two or more circles that have the same centre.

See **circle**

cone

A solid with a circular base, coming to a point at the top, similar to an ice cream cone.

See **solid, three-dimensional**

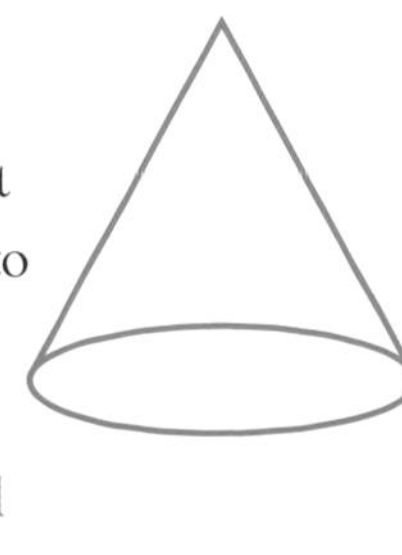

a b c d e f g h i j k l m n o p q r s t u v w x y z

congruent

Symbol ≅

Matching exactly in size and shape.

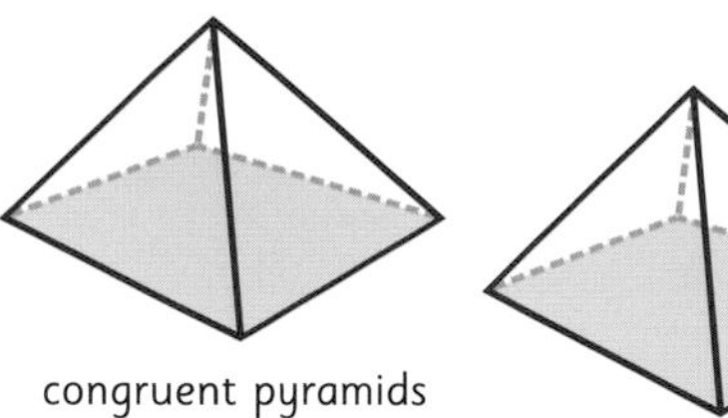

congruent pyramids

congruent triangles Two or more triangles with the same-sized sides and angles.

See **triangle**

corresponding sides A matching pair of sides in a congruent shape.

See **similar**

conjecture

A guess based on information that is complete.

consecutive numbers

Numbers that follow each other in a sequence.

1 2 3 4 5 6 7 8

See **sequence**

conservation of area

Keeping the same area, even though the shapes are different.

These three shapes have the same area of 3 cm². *See* **area**

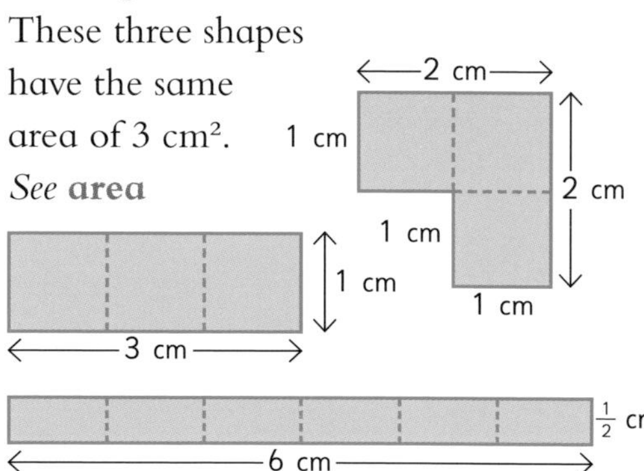

coordinates

A set of numbers or letters that shows the position of something. You use a pair of coordinates to find the position of a point on a flat (plane) surface, such as a map. The first number is the x-coordinate (how far across something is), the second is the y-coordinate (how far up something is). One way to remember which comes first is to say "along the corridor and up the stairs".

1. Coordinates can be plotted on a coordinate plane – a chart with an x-axis and a y-axis. The coordinates are written in brackets.

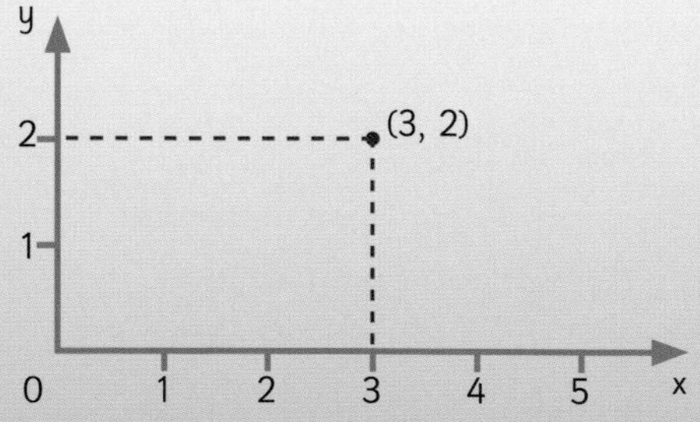

Point (3, 2) has the x-coordinate 3, and the y-coordinate 2.

constant

A number that always has the same value. The opposite of variable.

2c + 6 6 is the constant.

continuous data

Information (data) consisting of measurements that can be made on a continuous scale, such as temperature, mass, or distance.

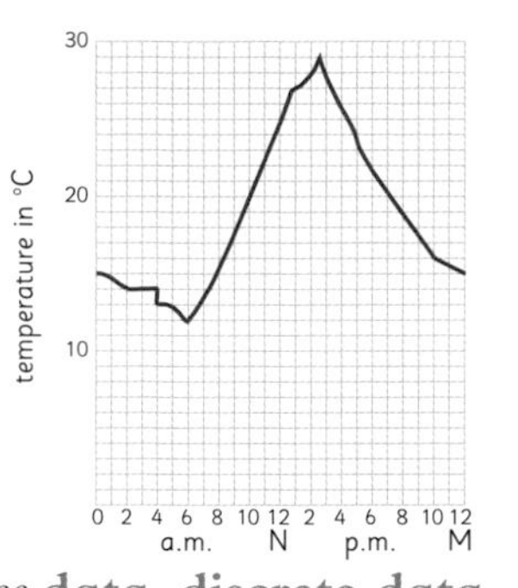

Temperature chart

See **data, discrete data**

converging lines

Two or more lines that meet at the same point.

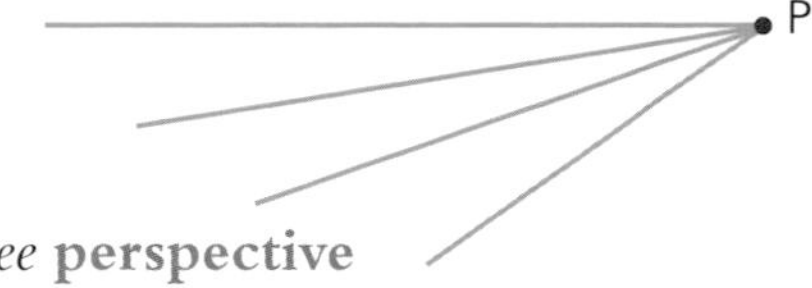

See **perspective**

convex

Shaped like the outside of a circle or a sphere. The opposite of concave.

convex

See **concave**

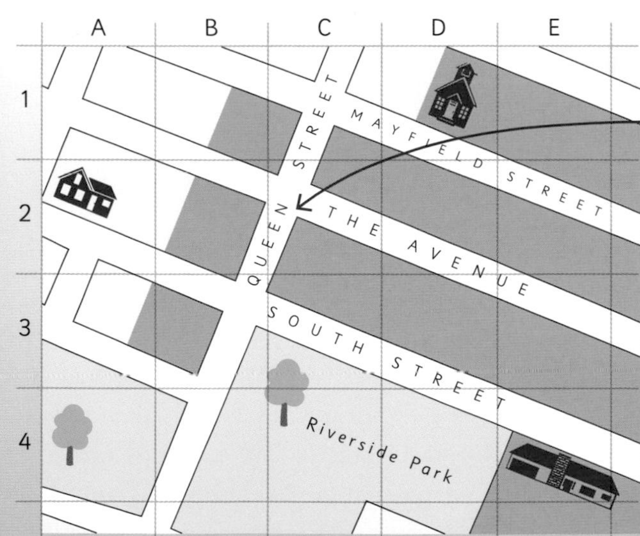

2. The position of the junction for The Avenue and Queen Street is C2.

My house is at A2.
My grandma's house is at D1.
My school is at E4.

See **axis, graph, intersection, ordered pair, origin**

correlation

A connection between two things.

correspondence

See **arrow diagram, one-to-one correspondence**

counterclockwise

Turning the opposite way to the hands of a clock. Screws and bottle tops are loosened counterclockwise.
Example If a clock is ten minutes fast, the hands must move counterclockwise 10 minutes.
See **clockwise**

counting

Giving one number to every item in a set. The numbers are in sequence.

counting number
All the positive whole numbers used in counting:

{1, 2, 3, 4... }

Zero is not a counting number.

counting system A way of finding out how many objects there are.
See **cardinal number, decimal, sequence, set**

counting principle

Multiplying the number of ways something can occur in order to find the number of possible outcomes.

Example
The café serves two types of pizza. You can choose one of four toppings.

cheese pizza

meat pizza

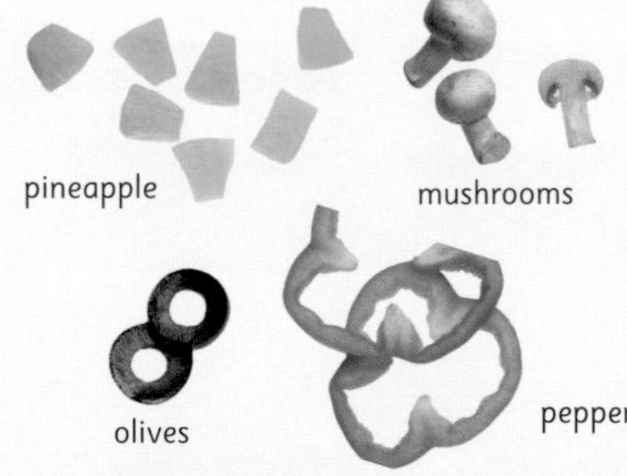

For each type of pizza, there are five options: one of four toppings, or no topping at all. Therefore there are 10 (2 pizzas × 5 options) options in total.

credit

1. A payment of money.

Example

His bank statement showed last month's credits.

2. An agreement that payment will be made at a later date for money, goods, or services.

Example

He bought a bed on credit.

See **debit**

cross section of a solid

A cut through a solid from one side to the other; a slice of an object.

Cross section of a lemon

See **face, front view, plan, plane, section, side view**

cube

A solid shaped like a box with twelve equal edges, six equal square faces, and eight corners (vertices).
A cube is a type of cuboid.

This is a diagram of a 2 cm cube.

edge
face
face
edge
vertex
2 cm
2 cm

This cube puzzle is made up of 27 smaller cubes.

See **cuboid, face, hexahedron, solid**

cubed number

When a number is cubed, it is multiplied by itself three times.

4^3 ← index, ← base

4^3 means $4 \times 4 \times 4$ or 64.
We read it as "4 cubed", "4 cube", or "4 to the third power".

See **index, power of a number, square of a number**

a b c d e f g h i j k l m n o p q r s t u v w x y z

cubic unit

The way volume is measured.

cubic centimetre A unit used for measuring volume.

1 cm^3 has a capacity of 1 millilitre.

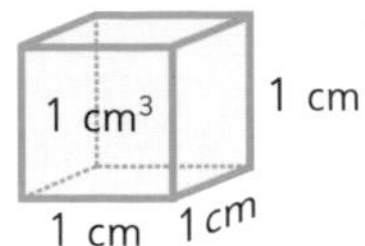

cubic metre A unit used for measuring volume.

1 m^3 = 1 000 000 cm^3.

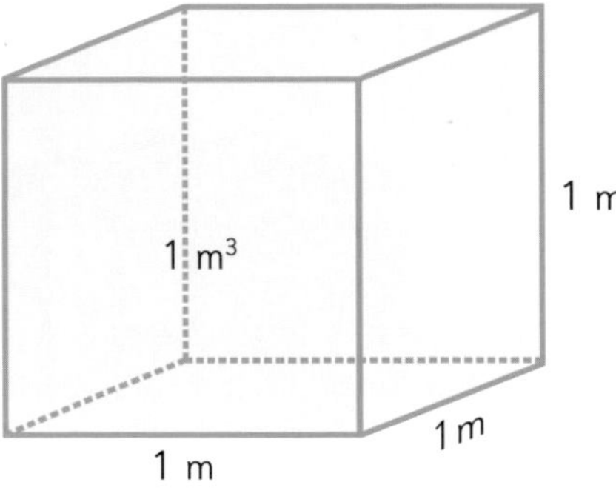

A cube with edges that are 1 metre long has a volume of 1 cubic metre. 1 m^3 has a capacity of 1 kilolitre.

See **capacity, cube, unit of measurement, volume**

cuboid

A 3-D, box-like shape, with twelve edges, six faces, and eight corners (vertices). The opposite faces are the same shape and size. Shoe boxes, cereal packets, and CD boxes are all cuboids.

See **cube, hexahedron, prism**

curve

A line with no straight parts. There are open curves and closed curves.

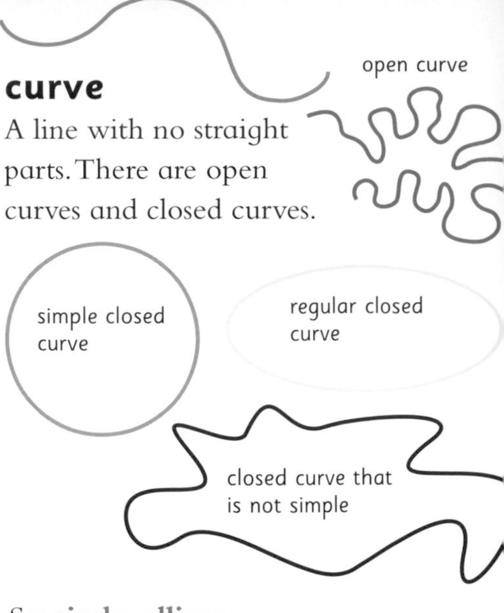

See **circle, ellipse**

customary measurement system

The main measurement system in the USA. It was previously used in Canada and the UK and called the imperial measurement system. We still use some terms occasionally, such as pint, ounce, and pound.

cylinder

A shape like a can. It has two circular faces at right angles to a curved surface.

See **right angle**

Dd

data
A collection of facts, numbers, measurements, or symbols.
Example Students' scores in a math test.

Jack	15
Yungjoo	16
Marcel	18
Isabelle	19
Joe	20

debit
An amount of money taken out of an account.
See **credit**

deca
Prefix that means 10.
decagram A metric unit of weight equal to 10 grams.
decalitre A metric unit of volume equal to 10 litres.
decametre A metric unit of length equal to 10 metres.
See **decagon, decahedron**

decade
Ten years.

decagon
A polygon (2-D shape) with ten sides.

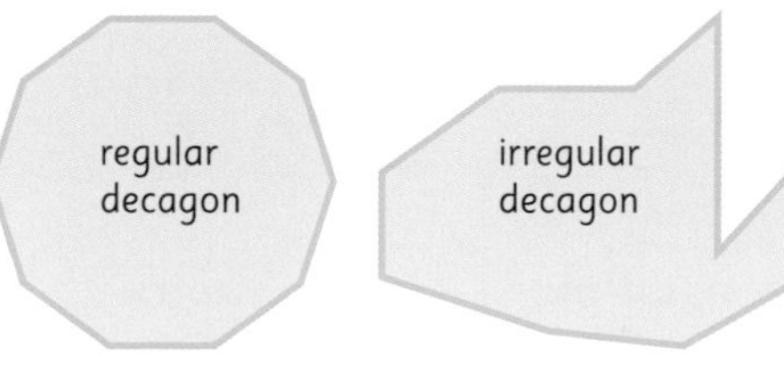

See **polygon**

decahedron
A polyhedron (3-D shape) with ten faces.
Example
This decahedron has been made by joining two pyramids and cutting off their tops.

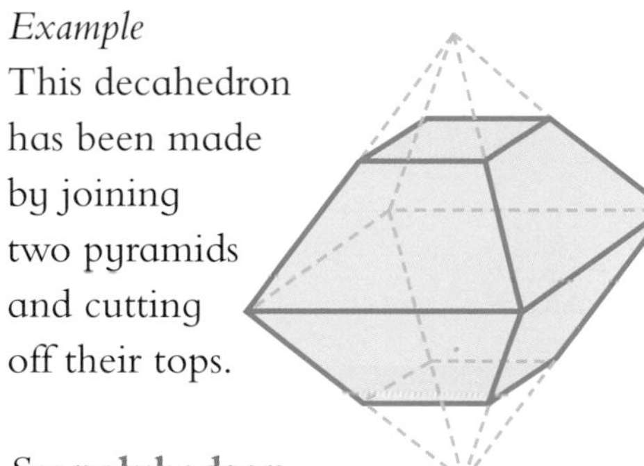

See **polyhedron**

deci
A prefix meaning one tenth.
decigram A metric unit that measures weight. It is equal to one tenth of a kilogram.
decilitre A metric unit that measures volume. It is equal to one tenth of a litre, or 100 millilitres.
decimetre A metric unit that measures length. It is equal to one tenth of a metre or 10 centimetres.

decimal

Containing 10 parts.

decimal fraction A fraction written as a decimal.

simple fraction $\frac{1}{10}$ = 0.1 decimal fraction

decimal place-value system
A system of numbers based on groups of ten. It is also called the base ten system or the decimal system.
The position of the digit shows the value of the number.
1000 is 10^3 and has 3 zeros after the 1.
0.01 is 10^{-2} and has 2 zeros before the 1.

10^6	10^5	10^4	10^3	10^2	10^1	10^0	10^{-1}	10^{-2}	10^{-3}
millions	hundred thousands	ten thousands	thousands	hundreds	tens	units	tenths	hundredths	thousandths

decimal point A point or dot that separates a whole number from a part of a number (a decimal fraction).
A comma is used instead of a point in many European countries and other parts of the world.

32.4
decimal point
7,62

See **base ten system, place value**

decrease

To make smaller or reduce.
To decrease something, you must either subtract a number from it or divide it by a number.
Example

The number of bottles was decreased from 3 to 2 by subtracting 1.
See **increase**

deduct

To take away. Another word for subtract.
See **subtraction**

degree

Symbol °
In geometry, a degree is a unit used for measuring angles.

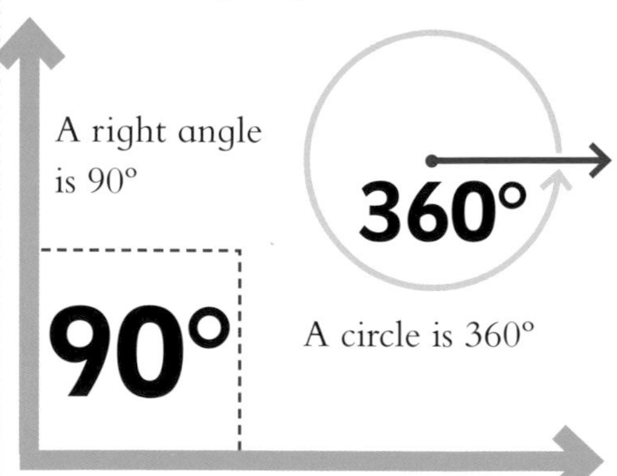

See **angle, Celsius**

denominator

The number written below the line in a fraction. It tells how many parts there are in the whole.

Example

This circle has been divided into 6 equal parts.

In $\frac{5}{6}$ the denominator is 6.

like denominators Denominators that match, a common denominator.

$$\frac{1}{8} + \frac{3}{8}$$

unlike denominators

Denominators that do not match.

$$\frac{1}{2} + \frac{3}{5}$$

See **fraction, lowest common denominator, numerator**

depth

How deep something is. Depth is measured from the top down, from the front to the back, or from the surface inwards.

descending order

Going down or decreasing in value.

Example

The following lengths have been arranged in descending order:

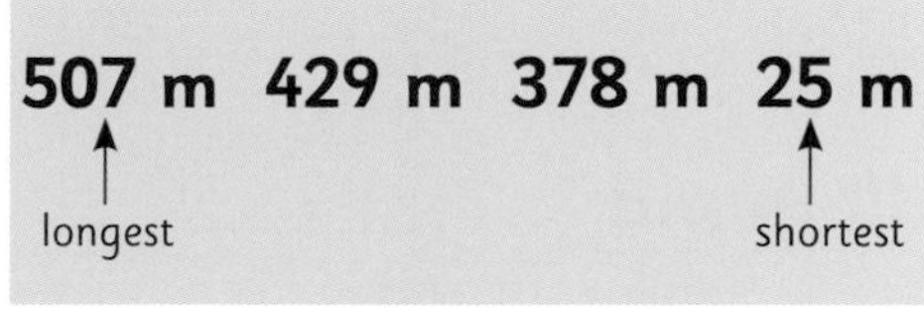

diagonal

1. Something that is slanting.
2. A slanting line joining two corners that are not next to each other in a shape.

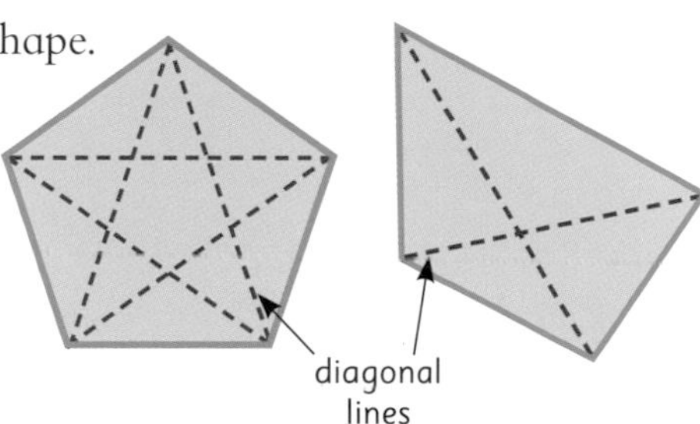

diagram

A picture that shows information.

Example A Carroll diagram shows how things are sorted into groups.

	black	not black
square		
not square		

diameter

A straight line that passes through the centre of a circle and reaches from one side to the other.

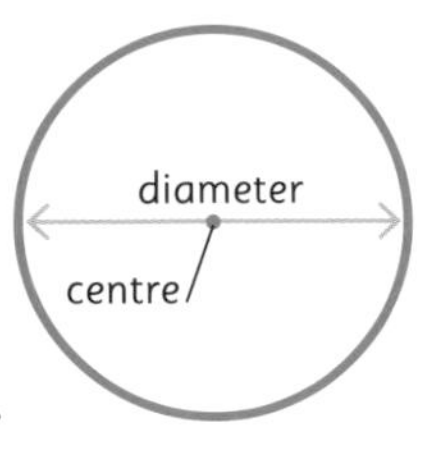

See **circle, line, radius**

diamond

A 2-D shape with four equal sides and four angles that are not right angles. The correct name is rhombus.

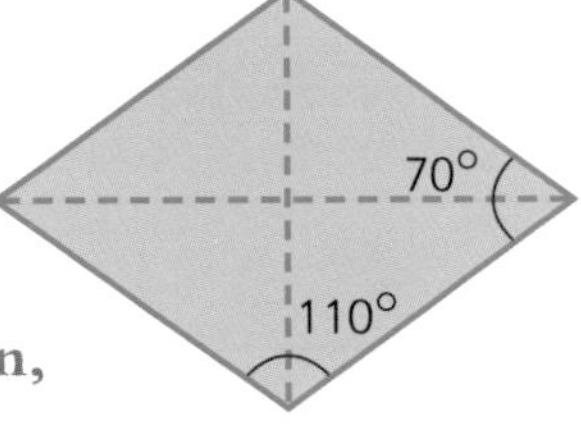

See **dimension, rhombus**

die

Plural dice

A regular 3-D shape, usually a cube, marked with spots or numerals.

One die

Two dice

Some dice have more than six faces.

difference

The amount one quantity (such as a number or a dimension) is bigger or smaller than another. You find the difference by subtracting the smaller number from the bigger number.

Example

$$10 - 3 = 7$$

The difference between 10 and 3 is 7.

dimension

WIDTH

HEIGHT

A measure of size including length, width, and height.

1. One-dimensional (1-D) objects have only length.
Examples lines, curves

2. Two-dimensional (2-D) objects have length and width.
Examples polygons, circles

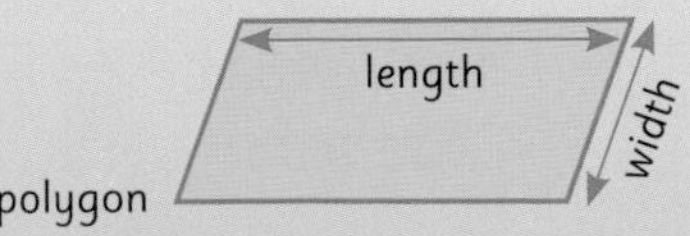

3. Three-dimensional (3-D) objects have length, width, and height.
Examples cuboids, pyramids

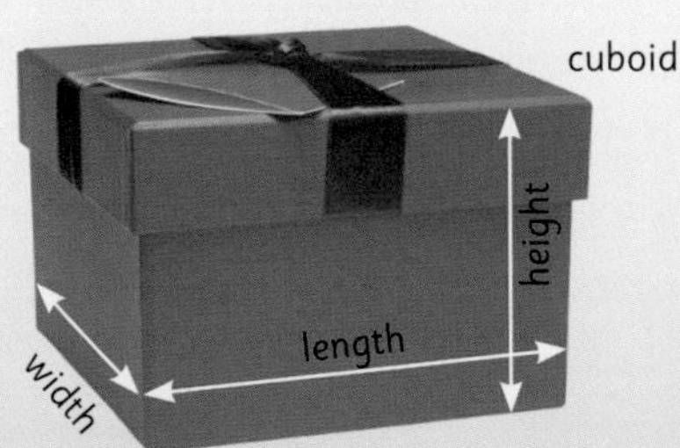

A point (dot) has no dimensions.

See **one-dimensional, plane, space, three-dimensional, two-dimensional**

digit
Numerals 0 to 9 are called digits. They are used to make other numbers.
Examples
56 is a two-digit number.
813 is a three-digit number.
See **place value**

digital clock
A clock or a watch that shows time by numbers. It has no clock hands.
Example
This clock shows ten to ten.
See **analogue clock, time**

dimension
A measure of size (see box, left).

direction
1. The way to go.
Left, right, up, down, above, below, inside, outside, near, forwards, backwards, etc.
2. Compass directions:
north (N), east (E), south (S), west (W), north-east (NE), south-east (SE), south-west (SW), north-west (NW).

See **clockwise, compass, counterclockwise**

direct proportion
See **proportion**

discount
If the price of something is reduced, it is sold at a discount. Discounts are often offered as a percentage of the selling price.

discrete data
A set of data that is based on counting. It deals with whole numbers (things that cannot be broken into smaller bits, such as goals – you can't have half a goal).

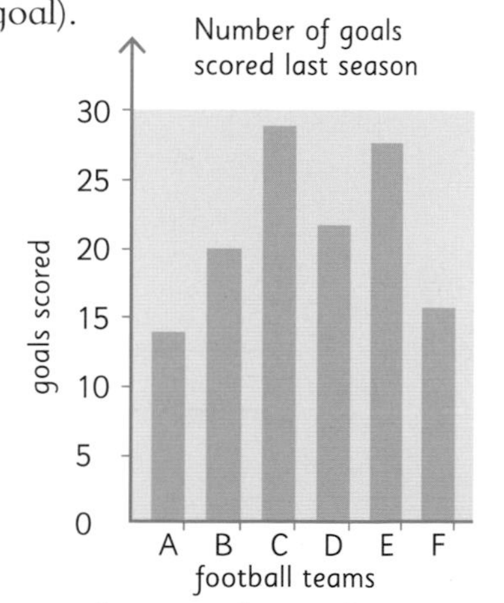

See **continuous data, data**

displacement

A change in the position of an object or of a quantity of material.
Example Dropping a die into water displaces some water.
The volume of displaced water is equal to the volume of the die.

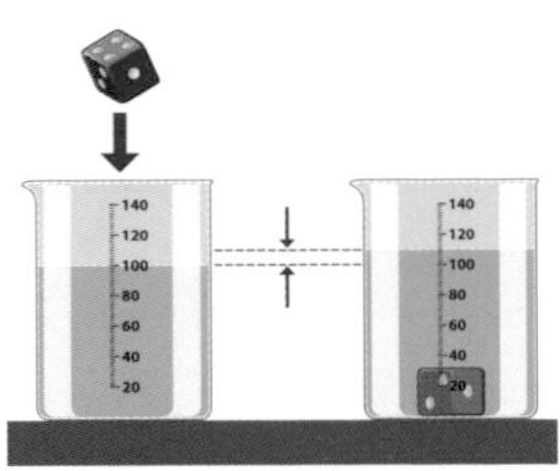

See **volume**

distance

The length between two points.

distribute

Give a share of something to each.
Example Mom is going to distribute the cakes.

division

Splitting a quantity into smaller, equal groups.
This can be done in different ways:

1. Grouping (quotition).

Example

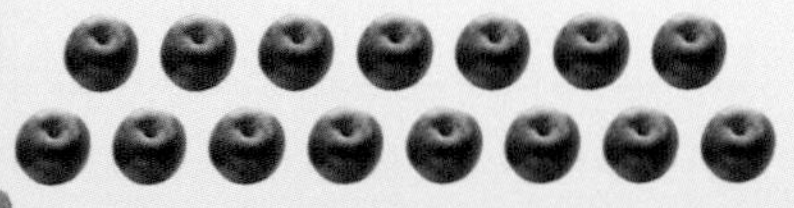

How many groups of 3 can be made with 15 apples?
The apples are to be placed into groups of equal size, 3 to a group.

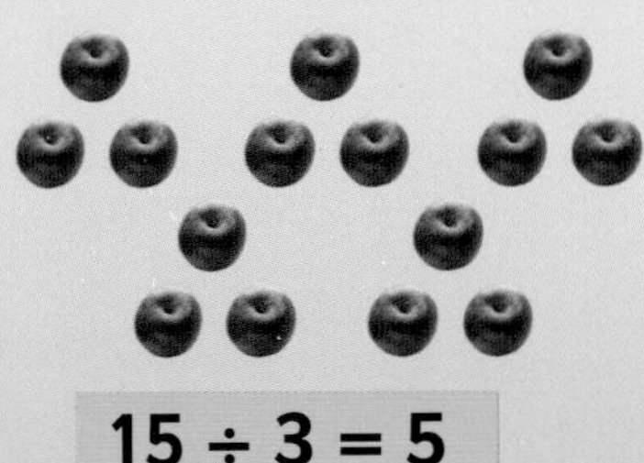

15 ÷ 3 = 5

There are 5 groups of 3 apples.

2. Sharing (partition).

Example
Share 15 apples among 5 children.
How many apples will each child get?
The apples are to be separated into 5 equal groups.

15 ÷ 5 = 3

Each child will get 3 apples.

3. Ratio (comparing quantities).

The ratio of juice to water is 1:5
(1 part juice to 5 parts water).

How much juice will you need for 100 ml of water? You divide 100 by 5 to find out. 100 ÷ 5 = 20. You will need 20ml of juice.

See **ratio**

distribution

See **frequency distribution**

distributive property

When you multiply a number by a two-digit number, this is the same as multiplying by each digit separately.

3 × 24
= (3 × 20) + (3 × 4)
= 60 + 12 = **72**

dividend

1. A number that is to be divided by another number.

24 ÷ 6 = 4

dividend, divisor, quotient

24 is the dividend.

2. What you receive as interest on money you have invested.

See **division, interest, quotient**

divisible

A number is divisible by another number if, after dividing, there is no remainder.

72 ÷ 9 = 8

72 is divisible by 9 and also by 8.

Note No number can be divided by 0.

divisor

A number that is to be divided into another number.

24 ÷ 6 = 4

dividend, divisor, quotient

6 is the divisor.

See **dividend, factors, quotient, ratio, remainder**

divisibility tests

A number is divisible by...	if...	Examples
2	the last digit is even	2, 4, 6, 122 , 358, 1,000
3	the sum of all digits can be divided by 3	261: 2+6+1=9 18: 1+8=9
4	the last two digits are divisible by 4	124: 24÷4=6
5	the last digit is 5 or 0	15, 70...
6	the last digit is even and the sum of its digits is divisible by 3	7,446: 7+4+4+6=21
7	there is no divisibility test	
8	the last 3 digits are divisible by 8	5,384: 384 ÷ 8 = 48
9	the sum of its digits is divisible by 9	3,123: 3+1+2+3=9
10	the number ends in 0	10, 20, 30...

dodecagon

A 2-D shape (polygon) with 12 sides.

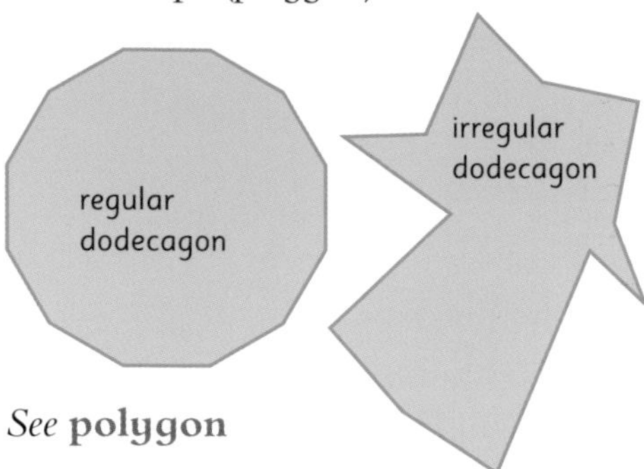

See **polygon**

dodecahedron

A 3-D shape (polyhedron) with 12 faces. A regular dodecahedron is made by joining together 12 regular pentagons.

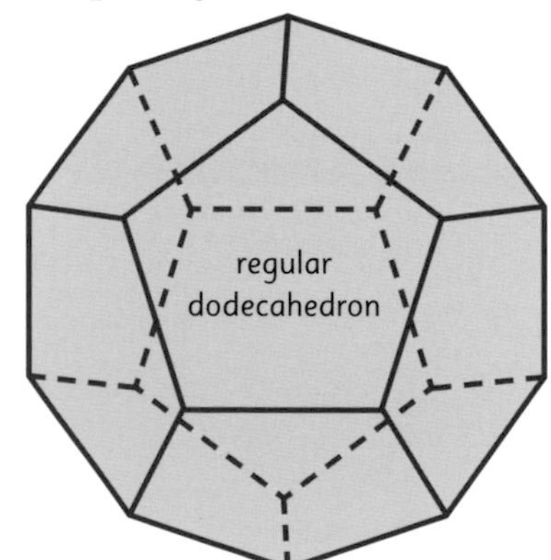

See **pentagon, polyhedron**

dollar

Symbol $

A unit of money used in North America, Australia, and New Zealand. It is divided into 100 cents.

See **cent**

dot paper

Paper printed with dots arranged in a pattern. It is used for drawing shapes, playing games, and to record work done on a geoboard.

Examples

square dot paper

isometric dot paper

See **geoboard, square paper**

double

Twice as many, or the same again.

double 8 is 16

10 is double 5

dozen

Twelve items.

One dozen eggs = 12 eggs.

Ee

edge

Where two sides (faces) meet on a shape.

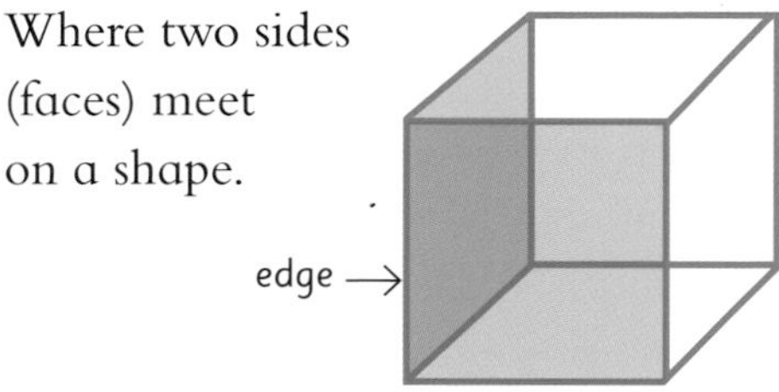

See **face, intersection**

element of a set

One of the objects within a set.

The blue triangle is an element of the set of shapes above.

See **set**

ellipse

A curved shape that looks like a stretched-out circle.

Example
A football is elliptical.

See **curve**

enlarge

To make something bigger.
This can be done using devices such as a photocopier, grid, or projector.
Enlargement is a common type of transformation.

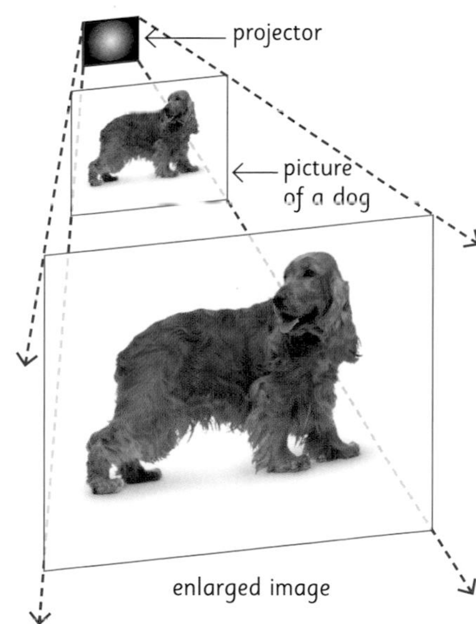

A projector uses light rays to enlarge a picture.

See **reduce, scale drawing, transformation**

equal

Symbol =

1. Identical in amount, or quantity. *Example* These two packets of sugar are of equal weight.

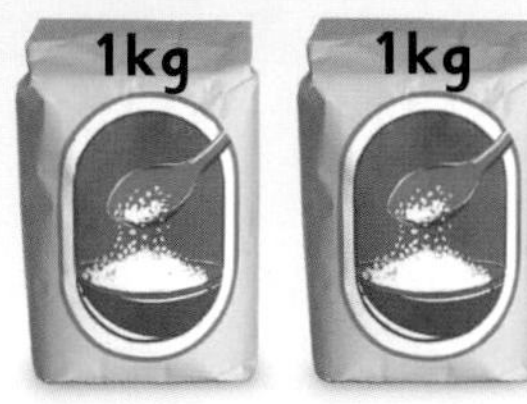

2. Of the same value.

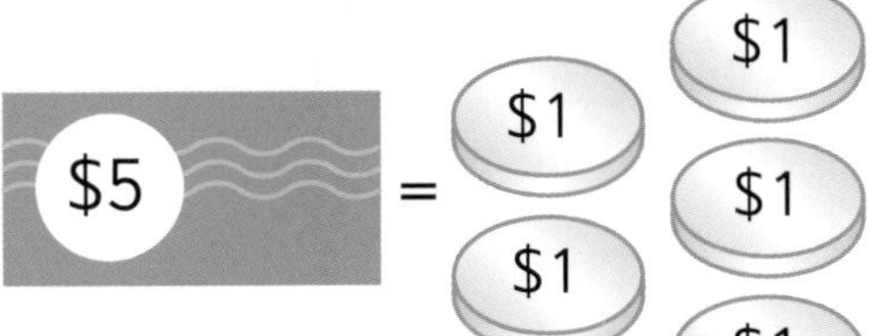

$5 bill = five $1 coins

3. Sums that express the same thing in different ways.

1 + 8 =   3 + 6 =
10 – 1 =   2 + 7 =

These sums are equal because they all represent the number 9.

equal sign The name of the symbol that means "is equal to" or "equals". It looks like this:

=

equality

Being equal. Having the same value, as shown by an equal sign.

2 + 4 = 6

See **equal, equation, inequality**

equally likely

See **probability**

equation

A statement that says that two amounts (quantities) are equal. An equation has two balanced sides, joined by an equal sign.

This equation is true only if x has the value of three:

x + 4 =7

See **equality, inequality, place holder, variable**

equilateral

Having sides of equal length. Regular polygons have angles of equal size and sides of equal length.

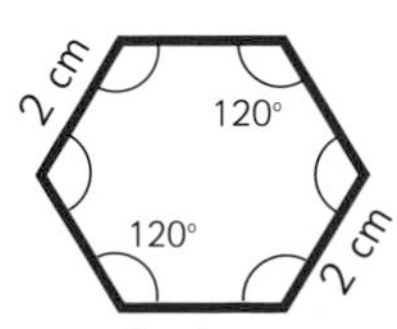

regular hexagon

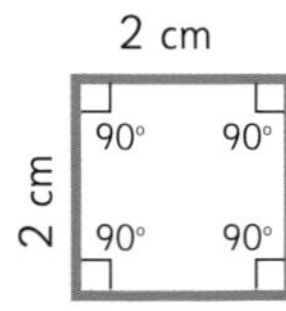

regular square

equilateral triangle A triangle that has three sides of equal length and three equal angles.
The angles of any equilateral triangle are always 60°.
See **triangle**

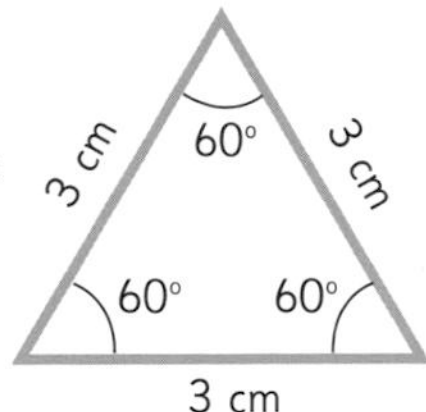

equivalent

Having the same value or amount. A $2 coin is equivalent to two $1 coins.

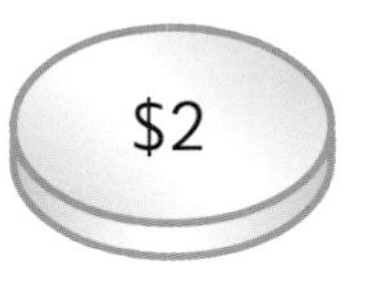

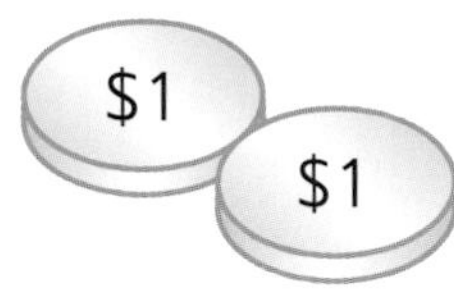

estimate

1. A rough or approximate calculation; a number that has not been calculated accurately. Estimated answers are often needed when working with decimals.
19.8 × 3 can be estimated as 20 × 3, so 19.8 × 3 ≈ 60.
See **approximation, calculate, rounding**

Euro

Symbol €
A currency used in many countries throughout Europe. It is divided into 100 cents.

evaluate

To find the value of.
The value of 21 × 3 is 63.

even

Equally balanced, equal in number or amount.

$5 = $2.50 + $1 + $1.50

even number

A number that is divisible by two. All even numbers finish with one of these digits:

0, 2, 4, 6, or **8**

See **digit, division**

event

A term used in probability. Something that can happen as a result of performing an experiment.
Example
The experiment is rolling one die. Many events are possible: rolling a 3; getting an even number; getting an odd number, etc.
compound event An event that involves the use of at least two items, such as rolling two dice.
dependent event An event where the outcome of one event affects the outcome of another.
Example
If you wake up late, you will miss the bus.
See **outcome, probability**

exact

Precise, accurate, correct in every way, not approximate.
See **approximation**

exchange

To give something and receive something else in return.
1. When we go shopping, we exchange money for goods.
2. Coins and notes can be exchanged for different coins and notes of the same value.

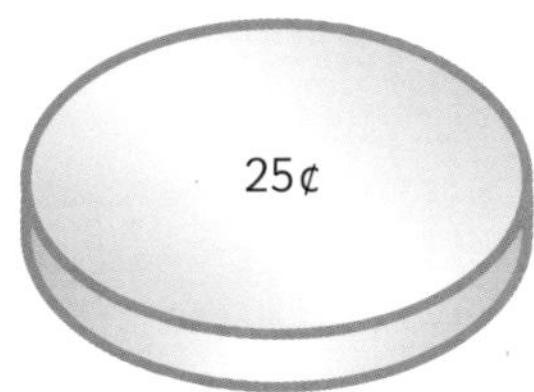

25¢ can be exchanged for two 10¢ coins and one 5¢ coin.

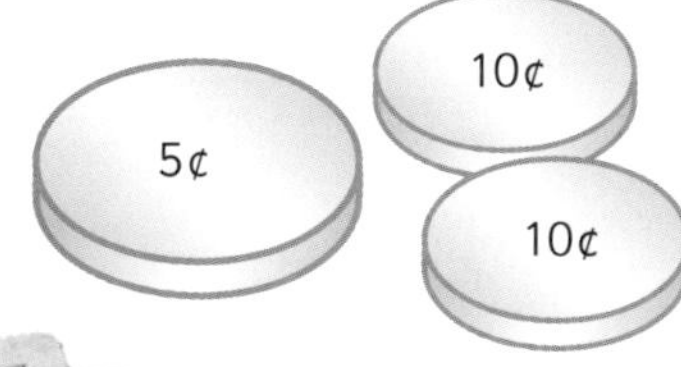

exchange rate

The comparison of values of money between different countries.

£1.00 = \$1.78

See **comparison, equivalent**

expand

Write out in full.

1. Expand 4

2. Expand 537

537 = 500 + 30 + 7

expanded notation

A way of writing numerals or algebraic expressions.

249 = 200 + 40 + 9
or
(2 × 100) + (4 × 10) + (9 × 1)

exponent

Another word for index.
See **index, power of a number**

exterior

The outside of something.
Example

Ff

face

In a 3-D shape, a face is the flat part of the surface that is bounded by the edges.

1. A cube has six faces.

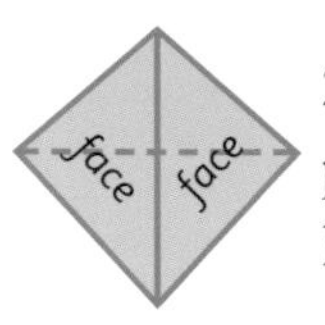

2. A triangle-based pyramid (tetrahedron) has four faces.

3. A square-based pyramid has five faces.

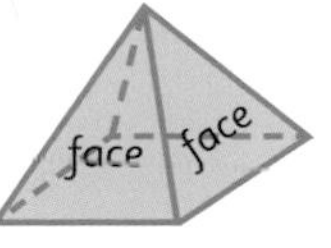

See **cube, edge, pyramid, tetrahedron, three-dimensional**

factors

All the whole numbers that can be divided exactly into another number.

	factor
$6 \div \mathbf{1} = 6$	1
$6 \div \mathbf{2} = 3$	2
$6 \div \mathbf{3} = 2$	3
$6 \div \mathbf{6} = 1$	6

1, 2, 3, and 6 are factors of 6.

The prime number 5 only has the factors 5 and 1.

factor

$$5 \div \mathbf{1} = 5$$
$$5 \div \mathbf{5} = 1$$

common factor A number that can divide both parts of a fraction exactly. It is used to help simplify a fraction.

greatest common factor The largest whole number that can be divided by each of the numbers in a fraction.

Example $\frac{4}{8}$

4 and 8 can be divided exactly by 2 and 4, so 2 and 4 are the common factors. The greatest common factor is 4.

$$\frac{4}{8} \rightarrow \begin{matrix} 4 \div 4 = 1 \\ 8 \div 4 = 2 \end{matrix} \rightarrow \frac{1}{2}$$

$\frac{4}{8}$ in its simplest form is $\frac{1}{2}$.

See **composite number, factor tree, fraction, prime number, whole numbers**

factor tree

A diagram showing prime factors – prime numbers that divide exactly into a given number.

18

2 × 9

2 × 3 × 3

prime factors of 18

See **prime factor**

Fahrenheit

A temperature scale in which water freezes at 32° and boils at 212°.
To convert from Fahrenheit to Celsius, subtract 32 and divide by 1.8.

false sentence

A sentence about numbers that is not true.
The open sentence
3 + ? = 10 becomes false if it is completed by any other number than 7. If it is completed by 7, it will become a true sentence.
See **number sentence, true sentence**

farthest

furthest
The longest distance away.

Name	Distance
Paul	3.50 m
Kate	3.89 m
Mike	3.47 m

figure

Another name for a numeral, line, shape, or solid.
1. Thirty-six written in figures is 36.
2. Half of this figure has been coloured in dark pink.

finite

Anything that has boundaries or can be counted.
1. The region inside a square is finite because it is bounded by sides.
2. The set of months in a year is a finite set because the months can be counted.
See **infinite, perimeter**

first

The one at the beginning, before any other.

Starting from the left, the first doll is the biggest.

flat

Being in one plane only.

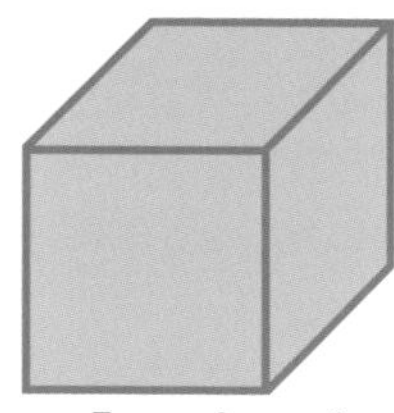
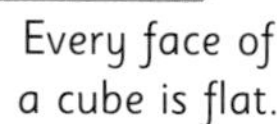

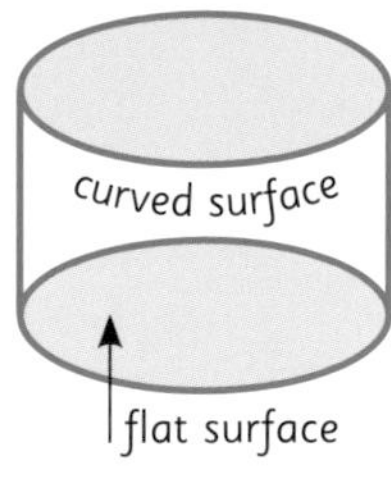

See **face, plane, surface**

flip

To turn over.

See **reflection**

This playing card has been flipped over.

flowchart

A way of describing a problem-solving rule using symbols.

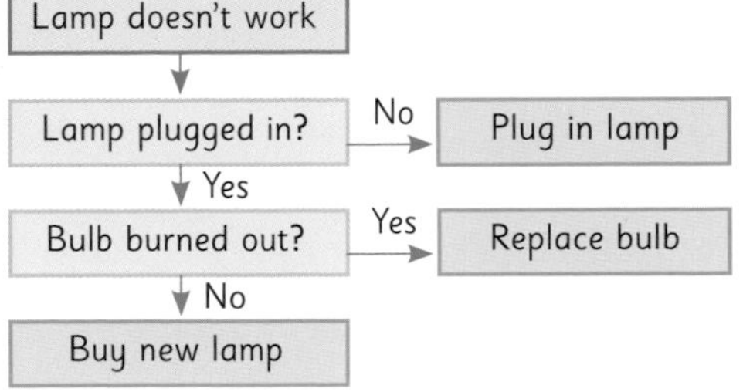

See **algorithm**

foot

Plural feet

Symbols ', ft

An imperial measure of length.

1 foot = 12 inches

To compare feet to a metric measure:

1 foot ≈ 30 centimetres

See **imperial measures, metric system**

formula

Plural formulas, formulae

An equation that uses symbols to represent a statement.

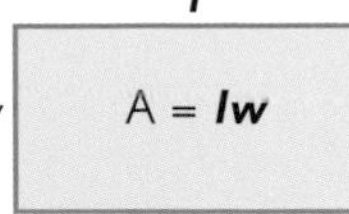

The area of a rectangle is its length (*l*) multiplied by its width (*w*).

See **area, equation**

fraction

A part of a whole quantity or number.

Examples

The fraction $\frac{1}{6}$ means 1 part out of 6 equal parts. One sixth ($\frac{1}{6}$) of the pizza is missing.

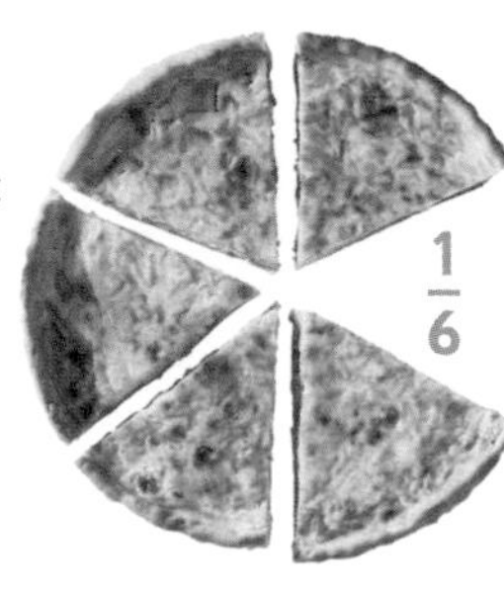

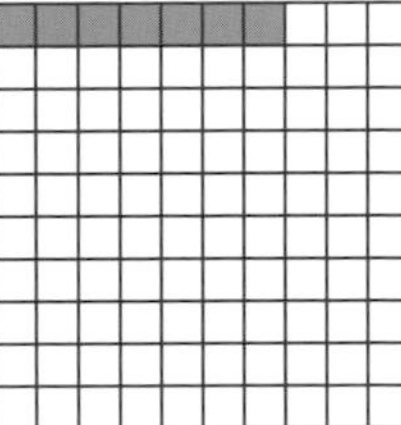

7 parts out of 100 parts are coloured in. The fraction is $\frac{7}{100}$.

Show $\frac{3}{4}$ of 8.

$$\frac{6}{8} = \frac{3}{4}$$

simple fraction A fraction with a numerator and denominator that are whole numbers. Also called a common fraction.

numerator ⟶ $\frac{4}{5}$ ⟵ denominator

simplest form A fraction is in its simplest form when its numerator and denominator have no common factors other than 1.

$\frac{4}{16}$ reduced to its simplest form is $\frac{1}{4}$.

See **decimal fraction, factors, improper fraction, proper fraction**

frequency

The number of times an item occurs in a collection of data.

Example

We tossed a die 50 times and recorded the number for each throw. We kept a tally of the 50 scores.

Number	Tally	Frequency
1	卌 II	7
2	卌 卌 II	12
3	卌 IIII	9
4	卌 III	8
5	卌 I	6
6	卌 III	8

Number 2 had the highest frequency. Number 5 had the lowest frequency.

See **data, frequency distribution, tally**

frequency distribution

A graph or table showing how often an event or quantity occurs.

Example

A frequency distribution table of marks for a math test within a class:

Mark	Tally	Frequency
20-29	I	1
30-39	卌	5
40-49	卌 IIII	9
50-59	卌 III	8
60-69	卌	5
70-79	III	3
80-89	I	1
	Total	**32**

frequency table

See **frequency distribution**

front view

A diagram of an object as seen from directly in front of it.

A front view of a house.

See **plan, side view**

Gg

gallon

An imperial measure of volume.

1 gallon ≈ 4.5 litres

geoboard

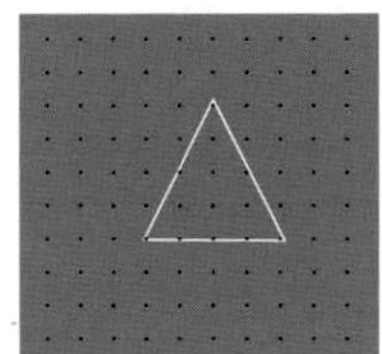

A board studded with nails that form a pattern or grid, usually of squares or equilateral triangles. You pull elastic bands around the nails to make shapes.

See **equilateral triangle, grid, pattern**

geometry

The part of mathematics that deals with solids, surfaces, lines, angles, and space.

See **measure, solid, space, surface**

geostrips

Strips of plastic, metal, or cardboard with holes equally spaced down the centre of the strips. They are used for making shapes.

shapes made using geostrips

googol

A very large number. It has the numeral 1 with one hundred zeros after it.

1 000 000 000 000 000 000 000 000...

graduated

Marked off with measurements.

Examples

A ruler is graduated in centimetres or inches.

ruler

thermometer

A thermometer is graduated in degrees.

gram

Symbol g

A unit of mass.

1000 g = 1 kg

The mass of this box of cereal is 250 grams.

See **mass, unit of measurement**

graph

A drawing or diagram that combines information about several things. There are different types of graph.

bar graph Horizontal or vertical bars used to show information.

A bar graph with vertical bars or columns is also called a column graph.

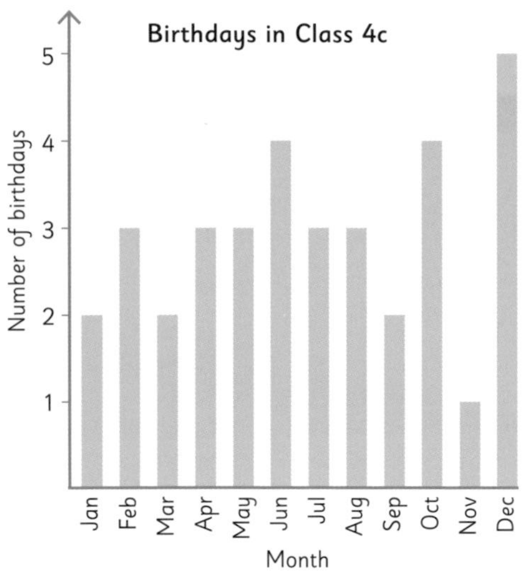

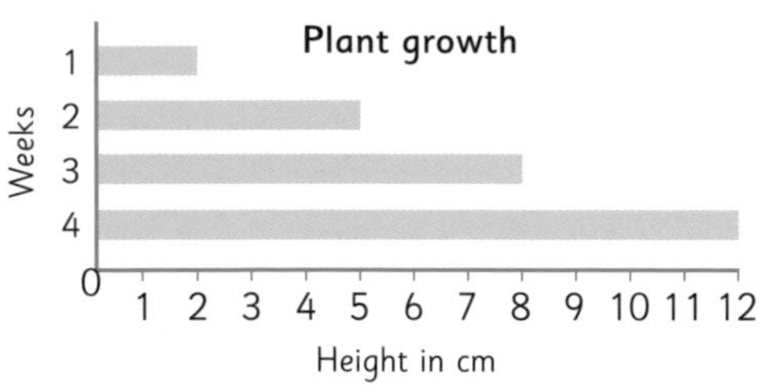

circle graph (pie graph, pie chart) A circle divided into sections to show information.

histogram A column graph with no spaces between the columns.

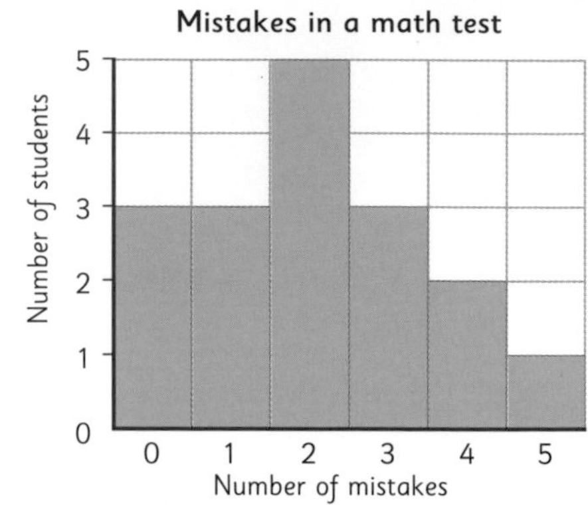

line graph A graph where you plot points then join them together to show information.

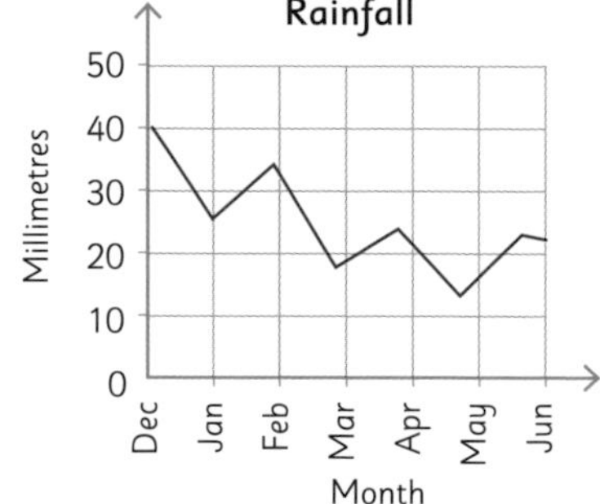

pictograph A graph where pictures represent real objects. Also known as picture graph or pictogram.

Class 7b – Favourite fruit

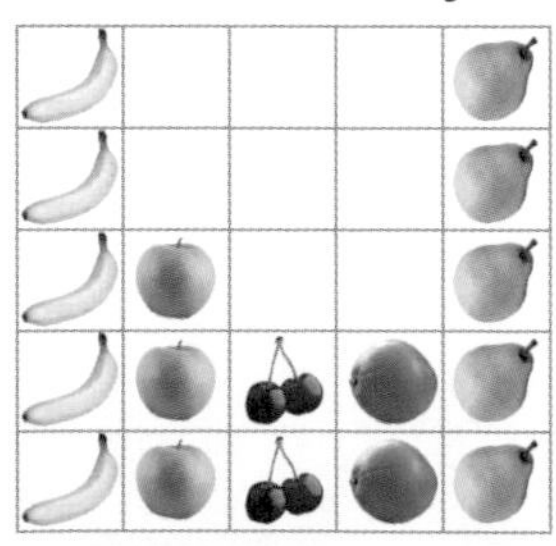

KEY:
1 picture stands for 1 person who prefers that fruit

graph paper

See **square paper**

greater than

Symbol >

More than, bigger than.

An expression that shows which number is larger in a pair of numbers.

7 > 6

7 is greater than 6

See **inequality, less than**

grid

Sets of parallel lines that cross each other at right angles. Grids are often found on maps and graphs.

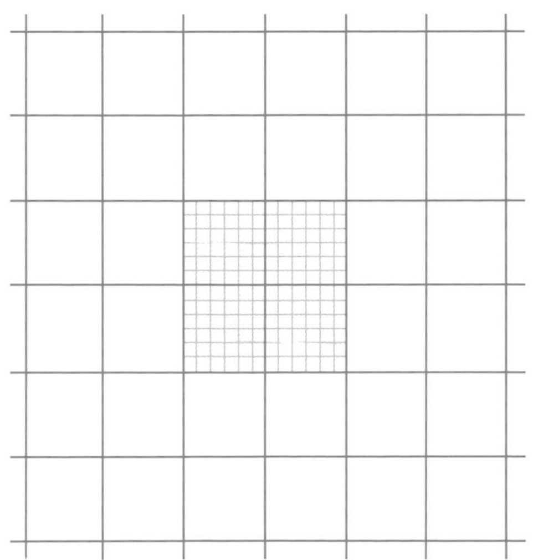

See **parallel lines, right angle, square paper**

gross

Twelve dozen (12 × 12); 144.

group

1. Putting things together in a set or group. In the decimal system, things are grouped into tens.

hundreds	tens	units
2	4	3

243 = 2 groups of 100
4 groups of 10
3 groups of 1

2. Two or more things.

a group of boys

grouping Putting things together into sets with the same number in each set. This is also called quotition.

How many groups of four can be made with twenty balls?

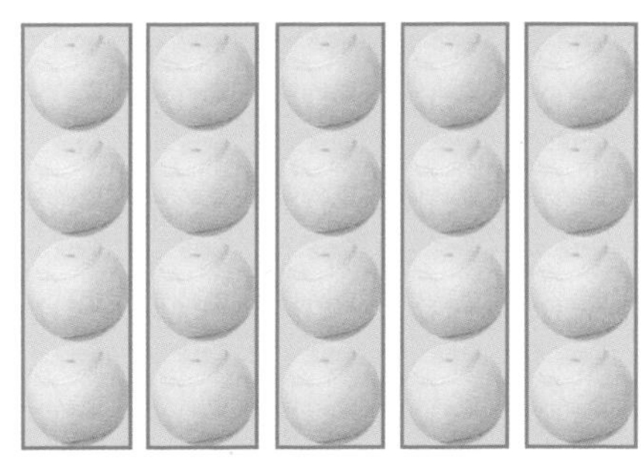

The answer is five groups of four.

See **division, set**

Hh

half

Plural halves

One part of two equal parts.

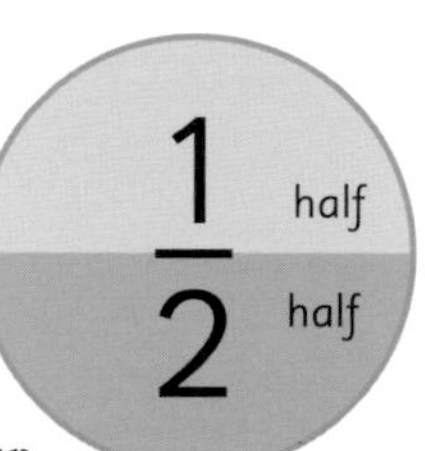

1. Half of a circle.
2. Half of twenty-four is twelve. $\frac{1}{2} \times 24 = 12$
3. This orange has been cut into two halves.

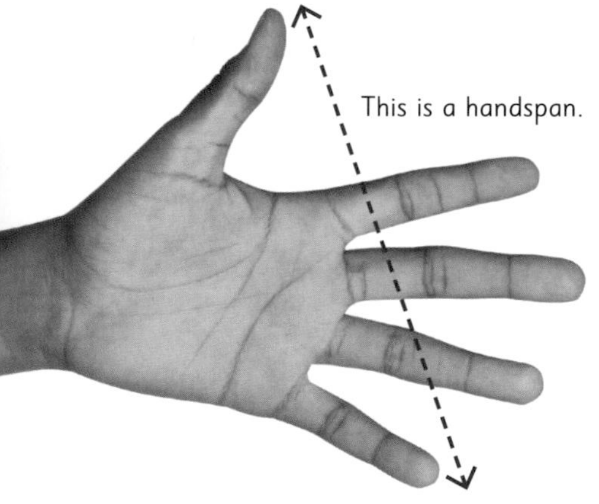

handspan

The distance between the thumb tip and the smallest finger tip on an outstretched hand.

A handspan is used as a rough measure for estimating the lengths, heights, or widths of objects.

See **arbitrary unit, estimate**

hecta, hecto

A term meaning 100 that is added to the beginning of a word.

hectare *Symbol* ha

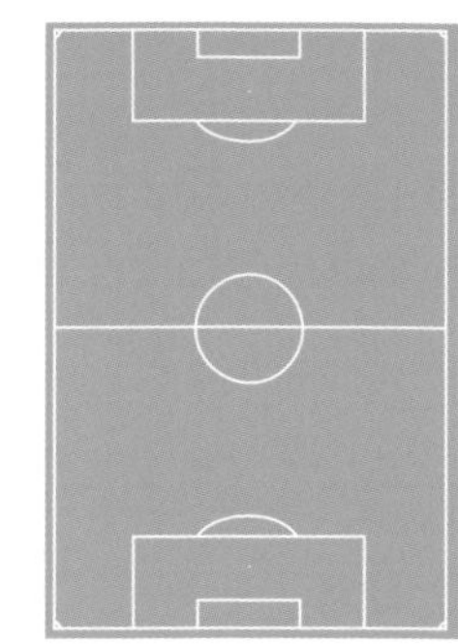

A metric unit of area. One hectare is the area of a square with sides of 100 metres. The area of a soccer field is approximately half a hectare.

hectogram A metric unit of mass equal to 100 grams.

hectolitre A metric unit of volume equal to 100 litres.

hectometre A metric unit of length equal to 100 metres.

See **area, unit of measurement**

height

Symbol h

Measurement from top to bottom, the vertical distance.

See **altitude, vertical**

hemisphere

Half of a sphere. The Earth is divided into the northern and southern hemispheres.

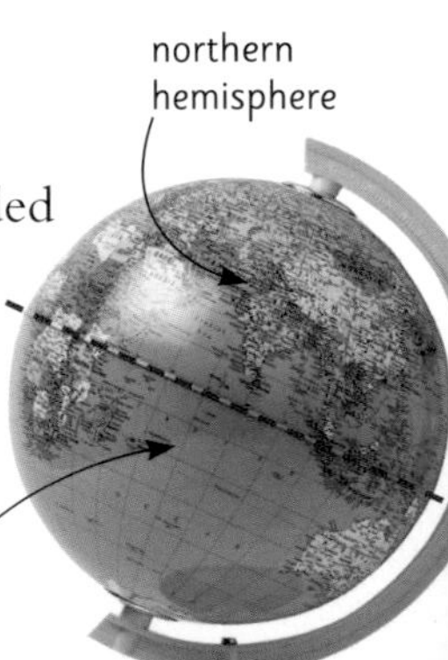

See **sphere**

heptagon

A 2-D shape with seven sides and seven angles. Regular heptagons have all sides and all angles the same; irregular heptagons do not.

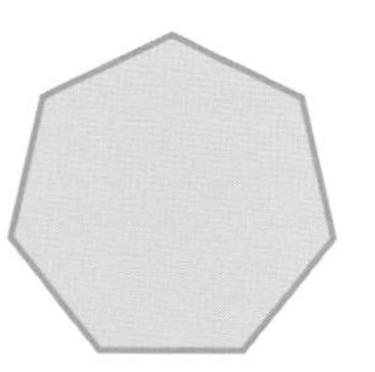

regular heptagon

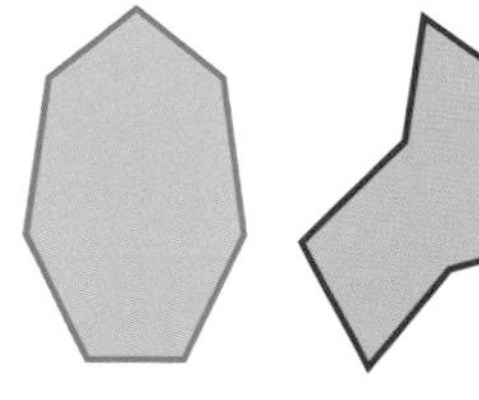

irregular heptagons

hexagon

A 2-D shape that has six sides and six angles.

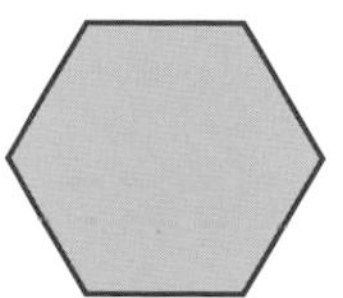

regular hexagon

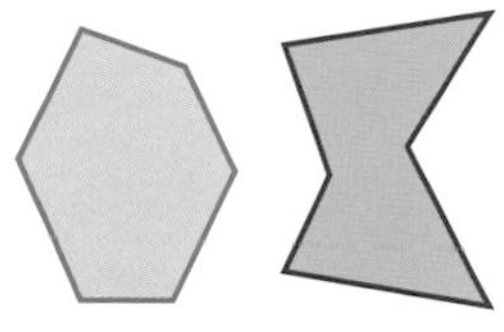

irregular hexagons

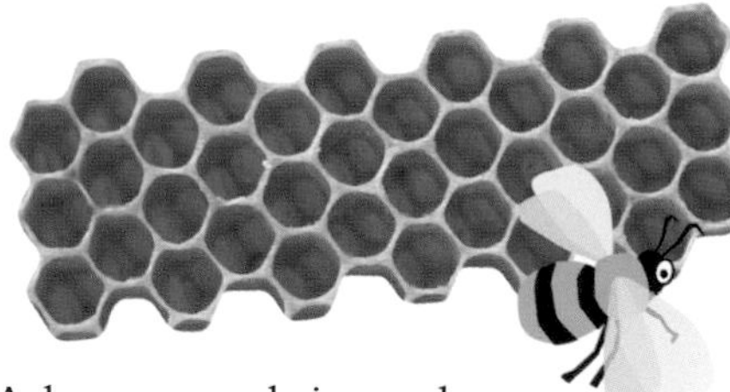

A honeycomb is made up of regular hexagons.

hexagram

A shape formed by two intersecting equilateral triangles.
See **equilateral, intersect**

hexahedron

A 3-D shape with six faces. All cuboids are hexahedrons.

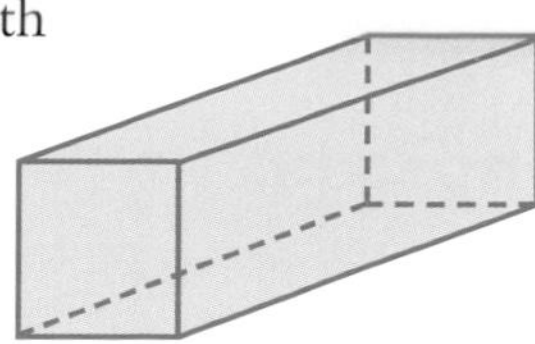

highest common factor (HCF)

Also called greatest common factor.
See **factors**

Hindu–Arabic

Our modern system of numbers. The symbols for all the digits, except zero, may have been developed as early as 200 BCE by the Hindus in India.

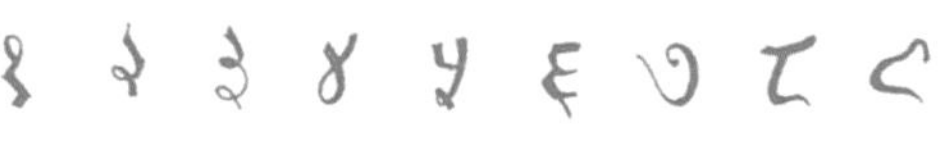

Hindu numerals

The Arabs adopted the system, and added zero.

Arabic numerals (13th century)

0 1 2 3 4 5 6 7 8 9

Hindu-Arabic numerals

The system has only ten digits, with zero as a place holder. The numerals, including zero, were standardized after the printing press was invented in the 15th century.
See **place holder, place value**

histogram

See **graph**

horizon

The line at which the land and sky appear to meet.

horizontal line

A line that is parallel to the horizon. A vertical line is at a right angle to the horizon.

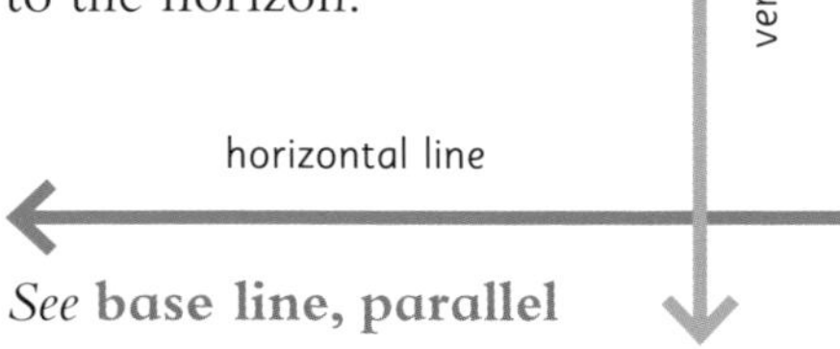

See **base line, parallel lines, right angle, vertical**

horizontal surface

Any surface that is parallel to the horizon.

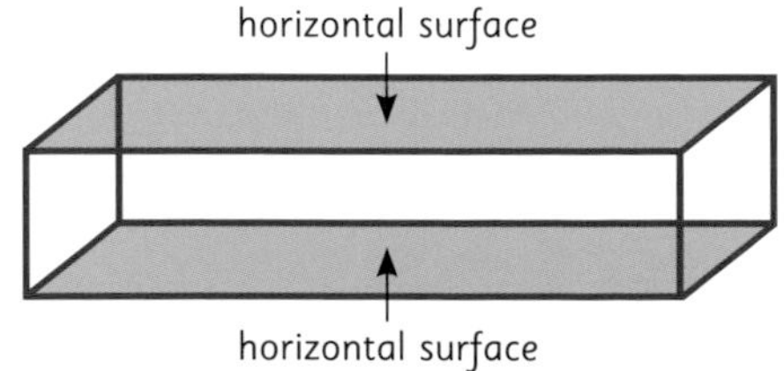

See **horizon, parallel lines, surface**

hour

See **time**

hundred

100 = 10 × 10

hundredth

$\frac{1}{100} = 1 \div 100$

hundred thousand

100 000 = 100 × 1000

hundred thousandth

$\frac{1}{100\,000} = 1 \div 100\,000$

See **decimal**

hypotenuse

The longest side of a right-angled triangle, which is the side opposite the right angle.

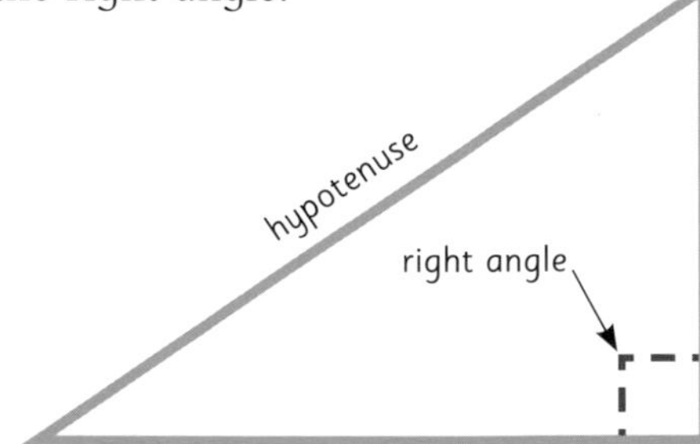

See **right-angled triangle**

Ii

icosahedron

A 3-D shape with twenty faces. A regular icosahedron is formed by joining together twenty identical equilateral triangles.

See **polyhedron**

identity property of multiplication

See **multiplication**

image

An exact copy of an object.

See **mapping, mirror image, reflection**

imperial system

Units of measurement that were used in Canada before the metric system.

See **metric system**

improper fraction

A fraction whose numerator is bigger than its denominator.

$\frac{12}{10}$ ← numerator / ← denominator

inch

Symbol ", in

An imperial measure of length.

12 inches = 1 foot

1 inch = 2.54 cm

This is an inch.

increase

Make larger by adding or multiplying.

See **decrease, progression**

index

Plural indices

Also called the exponent. It indicates (shows) how many times a number has to be multiplied by itself to produce the answer.

base → 10^6 ← index or exponent

can be written as **1 000 000** or **10 × 10 × 10 × 10 × 10 × 10.**

You say **ten to the power of six**.

See **exponent, power of a number**

indirect measuring

Also known as shadow-stick measuring. Indirect measuring is used to calculate heights that you cannot measure directly.

Example

To measure the height of a tree, use a 2 m stick and measure its shadow. Then measure the shadow of the tree.

$$\frac{\text{length of tree shadow}}{\text{length of stick shadow}} \times \text{stick height} = \text{tree height}$$

$$\frac{3\text{ m}}{1\text{ m}} \times 2\text{ m} = 6\text{ m (height of tree)}$$

See **ratio**

inequality

Where one quantity is less than or greater than another. In a math sentence, the following signs are used:

$<$ less than $\neq$ not equal to

$\leq$ less than or equal to

$>$ greater than

$\geq$ greater than or equal to

$$3 + 5 > 7$$

This inequation shows that three plus five is greater than seven.

See **equality, equation, greater than, less than, not equal**

infer

Come to a conclusion, or make a guess, based on observation or logic.

See **prediction**

infinite

Without bounds of size or number, unlimited, endless.

infinity *Symbol* ∞

Endlessness.

input

Data put into a number machine; the act of putting in data.

See **number machine, output**

insignificant zeros

Unnecessary zeros in numbers.

05.2 wrong **5.2** correct

integers

Positive or negative whole numbers including zero.

−5 −4 −3 −2 −1
negative integers

+1 +2 +3 +4 +5
positive integers

See **negative numbers, positive numbers, whole numbers**

interest

An amount of money given or charged by a bank.
1. The bank pays you interest for having money in a bank account.
2. Banks charge interest when you borrow money from them.

interest rate How much interest will be paid or given. It is often worked out as a yearly (annual) percentage of the amount saved or borrowed.

Oliver has $100 in his account.

The account has an annual interest rate of 5%.

At the end of the year, Oliver receives 5% of $100, which is $5.00.

See **annual, percent, principal**

interior

The inside of something.

interior angles Angles inside a shape. The sum of interior angles inside any triangle is 180°.

60°
30°
90°

30° + 60° + 90° = 180°

See **degree, exterior**

intersect

To cut across; to cross each other.
Example
The two lines intersect at point A.

A

intersection

1. The place where two or more lines meet, such as an intersection of two streets.

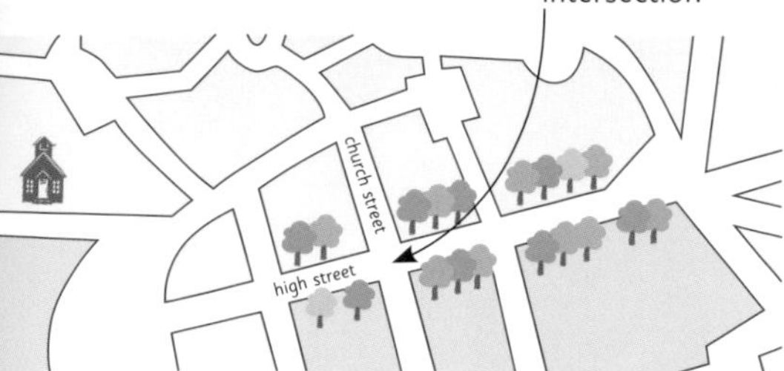

2. The region where shapes overlap.

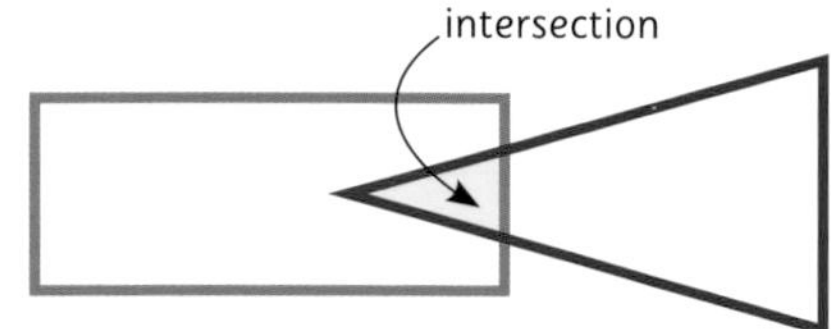

3. The set of elements in a diagram that are common to both sets.

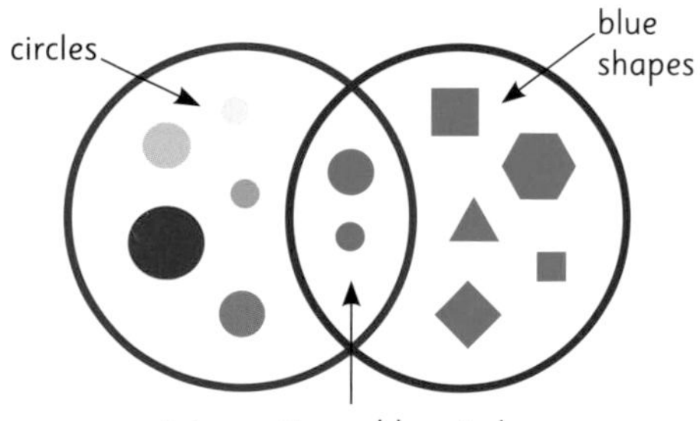

See **coordinates, origin, region, set, Venn diagram**

interval

The amount of time, or distance, between two events or places.

Example There is a twenty-minute interval between the two films.

inverse

The opposite or reverse of something.

inverse operation An operation that reverses the action of the original operation.

The inverse of addition is subtraction:

$4 + 3 = 7 \qquad 7 - 3 = 4$

The inverse of multiplication is division:

$6 \times 3 = 18 \qquad 18 \div 3 = 6$

See **addition, invert, operation**

invert

Turn upside down, reverse position.

Examples

$\frac{1}{2}$ inverts to $\frac{2}{1}$ or 2

$\frac{3}{4}$ inverts to $\frac{4}{3}$ or $1\frac{1}{3}$

irrational number

A number that cannot be written as a whole number or a ratio.

Example pi (π)

The value of $\pi \approx 3.141592643...$ but its exact value cannot be written down.

See **pi, ratio, rational number, whole number**

isosceles triangle

A triangle that has two sides of the same length and two angles of the same size.

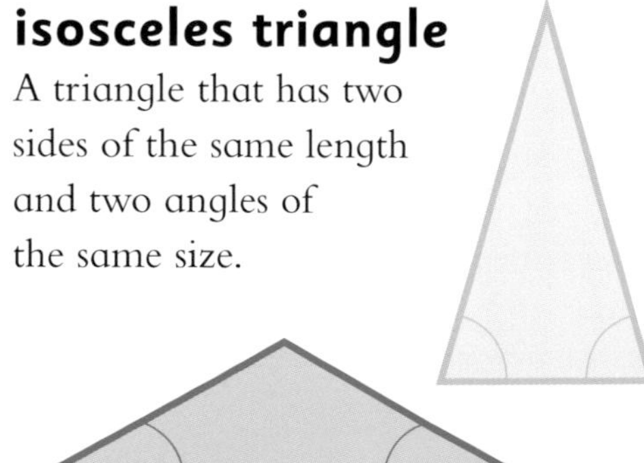

JjKk

joule

Symbol J

A unit of energy or work. It replaces the old unit, calorie.

See **calorie, kilojoule**

kilo

A prefix meaning a thousand.

kilogram

Symbol kg

The base unit of mass.

1 kg = 1000 g

The mass of potatoes in the sack is 12 kg.

kilojoule *Symbol* kJ

Used for measuring energy or work.

1 kilojoule = 1000 joules

This piece of cake contains 2000 kJ.

kilolitre *Symbol* kL

A unit of volume (capacity) for measuring liquids.

1 kL = 1000 L (litres)

Example

Five 200-litre oil drums hold one kilolitre.

kilometre *Symbol* km

A unit of distance. Distances between towns are measured in kilometres.

1 km = 1000 metres

See **distance, gram, mass, unit of measurement**

kite

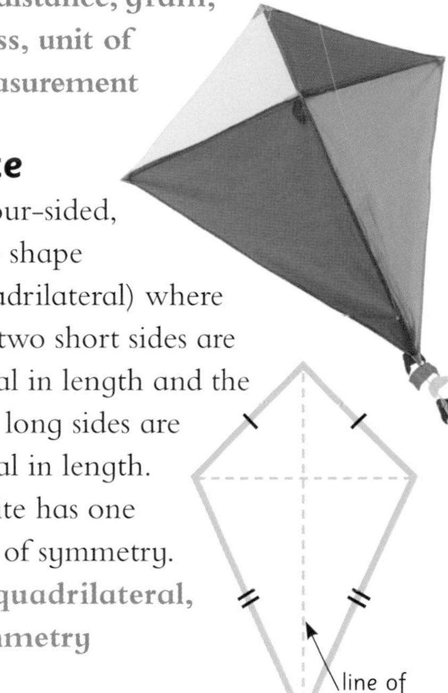

A four-sided, 2-D shape (quadrilateral) where the two short sides are equal in length and the two long sides are equal in length.

A kite has one line of symmetry.

See **quadrilateral, symmetry**

knot

Symbol kn

A measure of speed at sea and in flying, equal to travelling at a speed of one nautical mile per hour.

1 nautical mile = 1.852 kilometres

See **speed**

a b c d e f g h i j k l m n o p s t u v w x y z

Ll

leap year

A year with 366 days instead of 365 days.
It occurs every four years.
In a leap year, February has 29 days instead of 28.
You can tell if a year is a leap year by seeing if it can be divided exactly by 4.

1979 ÷ 4 = 494 (remainder 3)

1979 was not a leap year.

2020 ÷ 4 = 505

2020 is a leap year.

Century years are leap years only if they are divisible by 400.
These are leap years:

1600, 2000, 2400

These are not leap years:

1500, 1700, 1800

See **remainder**

least

The smallest thing or amount in a group.

The toy car costs the least amount.

length

How long something is from end to end.

1. The measure of distance.

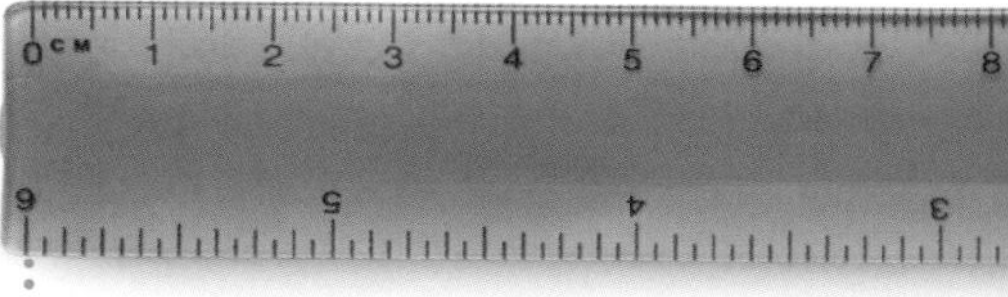

The length of this ruler is 15 cm.

2. An interval of time.

Example

The length of breaktime is 20 mins.

See **distance, interval**

less than

Symbol <

Not as much, smaller than.
An expression that shows which number is smaller in a pair of numbers.

$$5 < 7$$

5 is less than 7.

See **greater than, inequality**

like terms

Similar, resembling each other. Like terms can be added and subtracted, but unlike terms cannot.

like terms

unlike terms

See **unlike terms, variable**

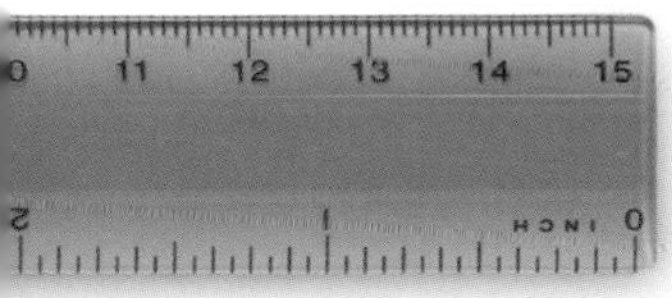

line

A thin mark with only one dimension. It can be straight or curved. A straight line is the shortest distance between two points.

line segment Part of a straight line.

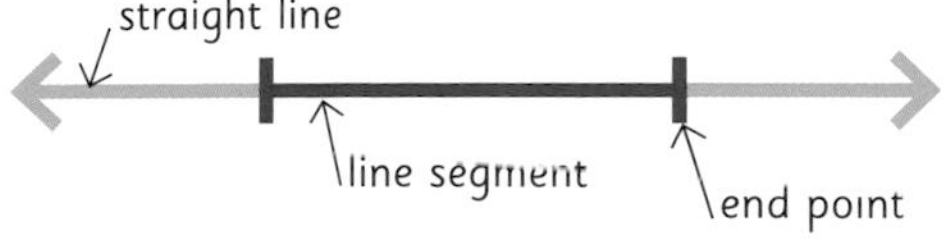

linear A measurement in one dimension only.

See **curve, dimension, horizontal line, vertical**

line graph

See **graph**

line of symmetry

Sometimes called the axis of symmetry, it is the line that divides something in half so that one half is the mirror image of the other half.

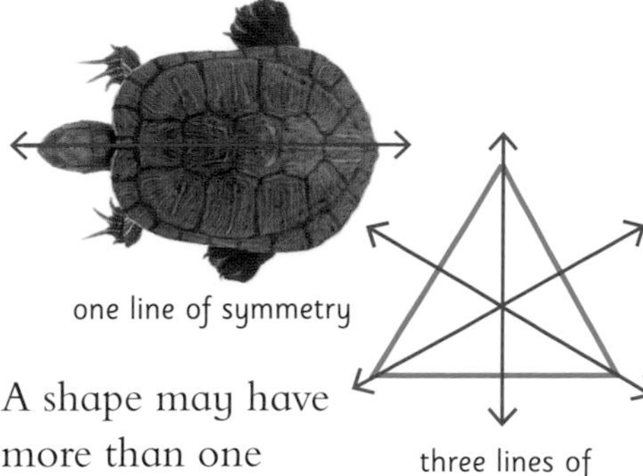

one line of symmetry

three lines of symmetry

A shape may have more than one line of symmetry.

See **asymmetry, axis, symmetry**

litre

Symbol L

A unit of capacity used to measure the volume of liquids or the capacity of containers. This carton of milk holds one litre.

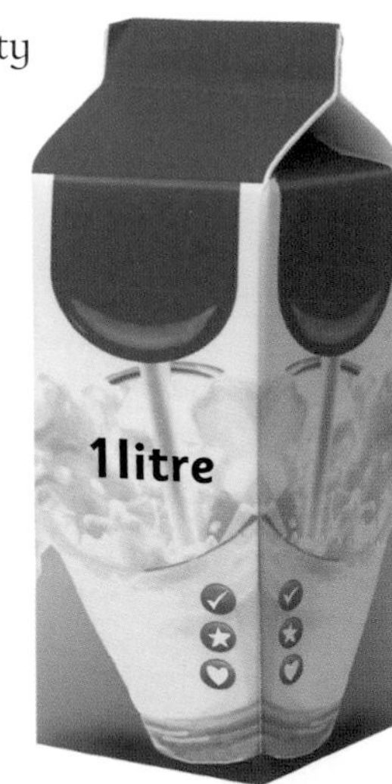

See **capacity, unit of measurement, volume**

loss

If the selling price is lower than the unit price, the seller makes a loss.

A car dealer buys
a car for $10 000
and sells the
same car for....................$9000

As the selling price of the car is less than the buying price, the dealer suffers a loss of $1000

See **profit, selling price, unit price**

lowest common denominator (LCD)

The lowest number that can be divided exactly by the denominators of two or more fractions.
Also known as the least common denominator in the USA.

Example

To find the LCD of

$\frac{1}{4}$ and $\frac{1}{10}$ ← denominator

you must find the lowest number that is divisible by both denominators (4 and 10). The lowest number into which 4 and 10 will divide exactly is 20. Therefore the LCD is 20.

Multiples of 4	Multiples of 10
4, 8, 12,	10, **20**,
16, **20**,	30, **40**,
24, 28, 32,	50...
36, **40**...	

● shows multiples of both 4 and 10

See **common denominator, denominator, fraction**

lowest common multiple (LCM)

The lowest number that can be divided exactly by two or more numbers. Also known as the least common multiple in the USA.

Example

What is the LCM of 2 and 3?

Multiples of 2	Multiples of 3
2, 4, **6**,	3, **6**, 9,
8, 10, **12**,	**12**, 15,
14, 16, **18**...	**18**, 21...

● shows common multiples of 2 and 3

Common multiples of 2 and 3 are 6, 12, 18... The lowest common multiple of 2 and 3 is 6.

common multiple A number that can be divided exactly by two or more other numbers.

See **division, multiplication**

Mm

magic square

A puzzle in which the numbers are arranged in a square so that each row, column, and diagonal adds up to the same total.

Example

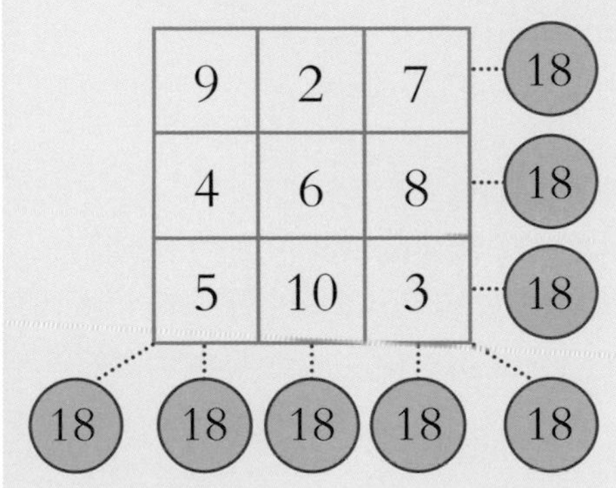

In this magic square, the columns, rows, and diagonals all add up to 18.

magnitude

The size of something, or how big something is.

many-to-one correspondence

See **arrow diagram**

mapping

A joining or matching operation between two sets. Each member of the first set is assigned to only one member of the second set.

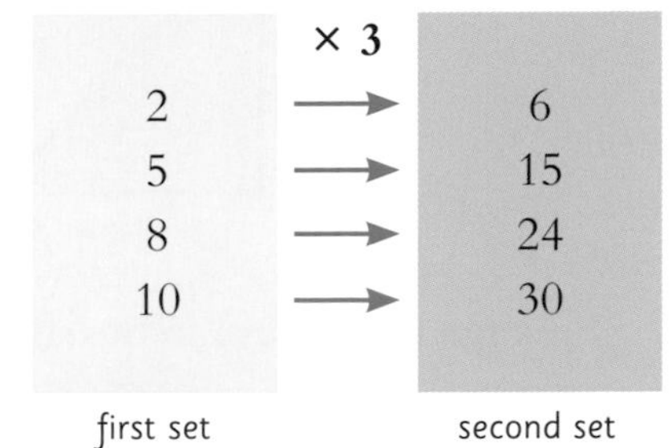

In the above example, 2 maps onto 6. 6 is called the image of 2.
See **arrow diagram, one-to-one correspondence, set**

mass

The amount of matter contained in an object. Mass is measured in grams (g), kilograms (kg), and tonnes (t).
This girl has a mass of 28 kg. The word "weight" is commonly but incorrectly used instead of mass.
See **beam balance, unit of measurement, weight**

matching

See **arrow diagram, one-to-one correspondence**

mathematical language

Instead of using long sentences, mathematics uses numbers, symbols, formulas, and diagrams.

Example

The shorthand

$a^2 + b^2 = c^2$

says the same as:

"On a right-angled triangle, the square of the hypotenuse is equal to the sum of the squares of the other two sides."

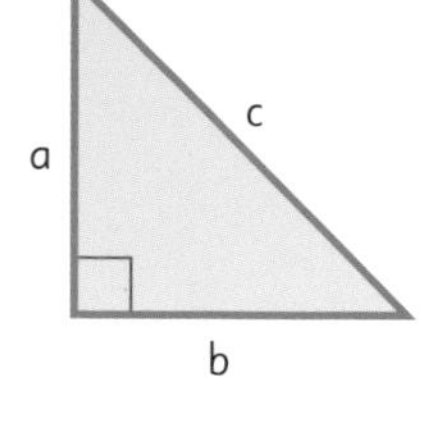

See **formula**

maximum

The greatest or biggest value.

Example The maximum temperature this month was 29°C.

See **minimum**

maze

A puzzle with a complicated network of lines or paths.

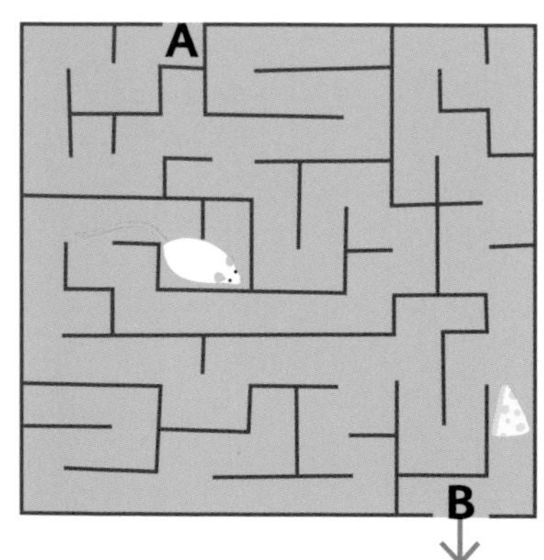

Follow the path from A to B without crossing any walls.

mean

The average of a set of numbers. It is found by adding up all the numbers and dividing the answer by the number of numbers.

See **average**

measure

To find out the size or amount of something.

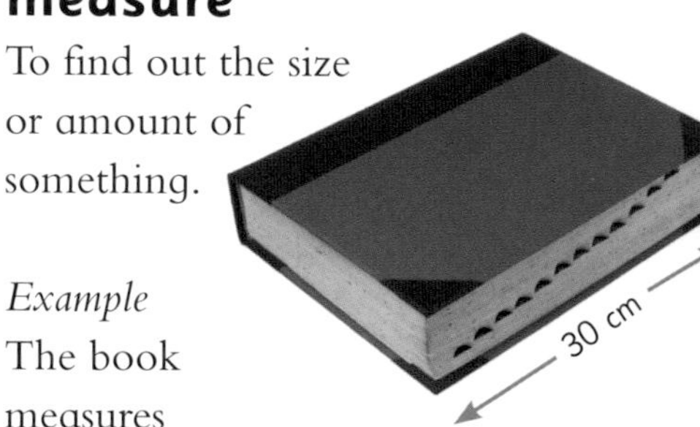

Example

The book measures 30 cm.

median

In statistics, median is the middle measurement or number, when items are arranged in order of size.

Numbers:

2, 2, 4, 5, 6, 8, 10

↑ median = 5

Where there is no middle number, an average of the two central numbers is taken.

Numbers:

2, 3, 4, 8, 9, 10

↑ ↑ median = (4 + 8) ÷ 2 = 6

See **average, mean, mode**

mega

Symbol M

A prefix (a word added to the start of another word) meaning one million.

megalitre *Symbol* ML

A unit of capacity.

1 megalitre = 1 000 000 litres

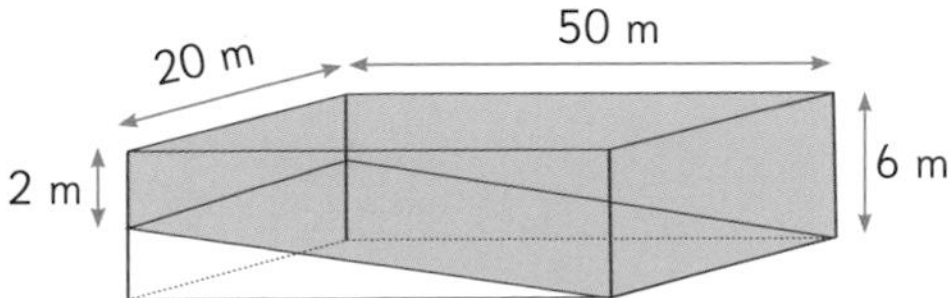

This swimming pool contains four megalitres (4 ML) of water.

metre

Symbol m

The base unit of length or distance.

1 m = 100 cm

1 m = 1000 mm

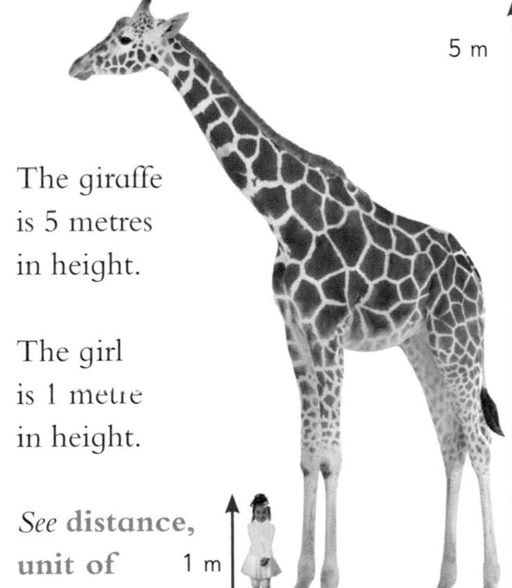

The giraffe is 5 metres in height.

The girl is 1 metre in height.

See **distance, unit of measurement**

metric system

A decimal system of weights and measures. The base unit for length is metre, for mass is kilogram, and for time is second.

See **imperial system, standard unit**

midpoint

A point in the middle of an interval.

The point M is the midpoint of the interval (or distance) AB.

See **bisect, interval**

mile

An imperial measure of length.

1 mile ≈ 1.6 km

mileage

The distance in miles a vehicle travels using a certain amount of gasoline. Mileage is measured in miles per gallon of gasoline (mpg). Mileage is also called fuel economy and can be measured in litres of gasoline per 100 kilometres.

milli

Symbol m

Prefix meaning one thousandth. $\frac{1}{1000}$

milligram *Symbol* mg

A unit of mass equal to $\frac{1}{1000}$ of a gram.

1 mg = $\frac{1}{1000}$ gram	1 mg = 0.001 gram

See **gram, mass**

millilitre *Symbol* mL

A unit of capacity that is equal to one-thousandth of a litre.

1000 mL = 1 litre

A teaspoon holds 5 mL.

This bottle holds 1 litre.

This bucket holds 9 litres.

Note One millilitre of water at 4°C has a mass of one gram.

See **litre, volume**

millimetre *Symbol* mm

0

A unit of length that is equal to one-thousandth of a metre.

10 mm

1000 mm = 1 metre

See **metre, length**

million

One thousand thousands:

1 000 000

millionth One part out of a million. $\frac{1}{1\,000\,000}$

minimum

The smallest or least value.

Example The minimum temperature in July was 4°C.

See **maximum**

minuend

A number from which another number is to be subtracted.

29 − 7 = 22

minuend (29), subtrahend (7), difference (22)

In this example, 29 is the minuend.

See **difference, subtraction**

minus

Symbol –

1. Subtract or take away. *Example* Eight minus two is written as 8 – 2 and means two subtracted from eight.

8 – 2 = 6

2. A symbol to mark negative numbers.

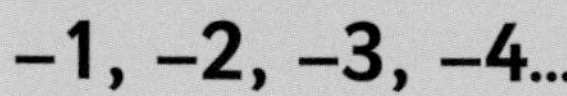

–1, –2, –3, –4...

Minus 1, minus 2, minus 3, minus 4...

See **integers, negative numbers, subtraction**

minute

See **time**

mirror image

A reflection, as in a mirror.

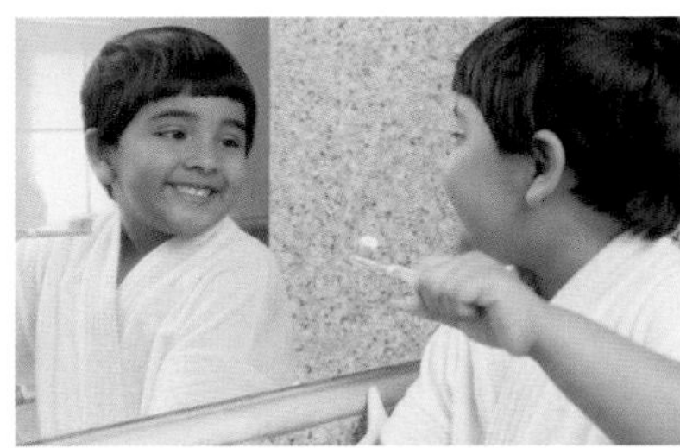

See **image, reflection**

mixed number

A whole number and a fraction.

$$1\frac{1}{2} \quad 3\frac{5}{6}$$

This is another way of writing an improper fraction.

$$\frac{3}{2} = 1\frac{1}{2} \quad \frac{35}{30} = 1\frac{5}{30} = 1\frac{1}{6}$$

See **fraction, improper fraction, whole numbers**

möbius strip

Also spelt as moebius.
A surface with only one side, made by half-twisting a strip of paper and joining the ends together. If you draw a line along the middle of the strip, when you come back to the start, you will have drawn on both sides of the paper. If you cut along the line, you get one big strip.

mode

In statistics, the number that occurs most often in a set of numbers.
For the numbers:

1, 1, 2, 4, 4, 6, 6, 6, 6, 7, 7, 7, 8, 10

6 is the mode.
See **average, mean, median**

model

A smaller 3-D copy of an actual or designed object.

This is a model of an airplane.

See **three-dimensional**

month

A period of time. A month has 28, 29, 30, or 31 days.

more

Greater in amount.
Example $4 is more than $3.

most

The greatest amount.
Example Anna has 20 cents, Ben has 35 cents, and Joe has 5 cents. Ben has the most.

multilateral

Having many sides.

multiplication

Multiply, multiplying.

Symbol ×

A quick way of adding up lots of the same number (repeated addition) or adding equal groups of things together.

The symbol "×" means groups of, or multiplied by.

This shows
2 groups of 3 eggs: 2 × 3 = 6
or, 3 multiplied by 2: 3 × 2 = 6
or, 3 made 2 times bigger = 6

multiple A number that can be divided exactly by another number.
Multiples of two are:

2, 4, 6, 8, 10, 12...

Multiples of three are:

3, 6, 9, 12, 15, 18...

multiplicand The number that is being multiplied.

identity property of multiplication When a number is multiplied by 1, the answer (product) is equal to the original number.

$$7 \times 1 = 7$$
$$1 \times 138 = 138$$

It can be used when converting a fraction to an equivalent form.

$$\frac{2}{3} = \frac{?}{12}$$
$$\frac{2}{3} \times \frac{4}{4} = \frac{8}{12}$$

The same as x 1

To convert $\frac{2}{3}$ to $\frac{8}{12}$, $\frac{2}{3}$ is multiplied by 1, or $\frac{4}{4}$.
We use 4 because 3 × 4 = 12.
The numerators (top numbers) are then multiplied, to give the answer $\frac{8}{12}$.

multiplier The number by which another number is multiplied.

8 × 7 = 56

multiplicand multiplier product

multiply Carry out the process of multiplication or repeated addition.

5 × 7 = 35

See **addition, division, fractions, lowest common multiple, operation, product**
See **multiplication square on p128**

Nn

natural number

One of the counting numbers.

1, 2, 3, 4, 5, 6, 7, 8, 9...

See **counting number, positive numbers**

nautical mile

A unit of length as used on planes, boats, and ships. A nautical mile is based on the circumference of the Earth. 1 nautical mile equals 1852 metres or 1.852 kilometres.
See **knot**

negative numbers

Numbers less than zero. Negative numbers are written with the minus sign (-) in front of them.

-1, -2, -3, -4, -5 etc
-0.1, -0.2, etc

Negative numbers on a number line:

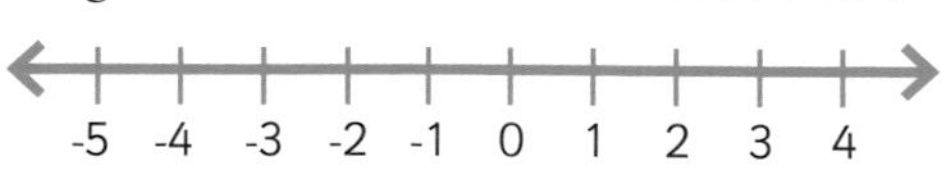

See **integers, minus, number line, positive numbers, zero**

net

A flat pattern that can be cut out, folded, and glued together to make a 3-D model of a solid.

Net of a cube:

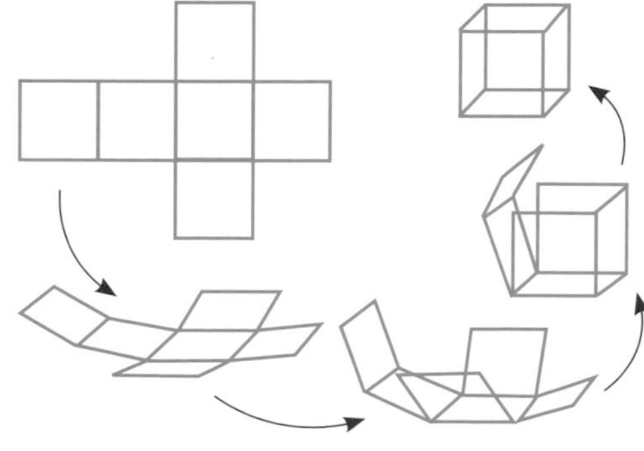

Net of a square-based pyramid:

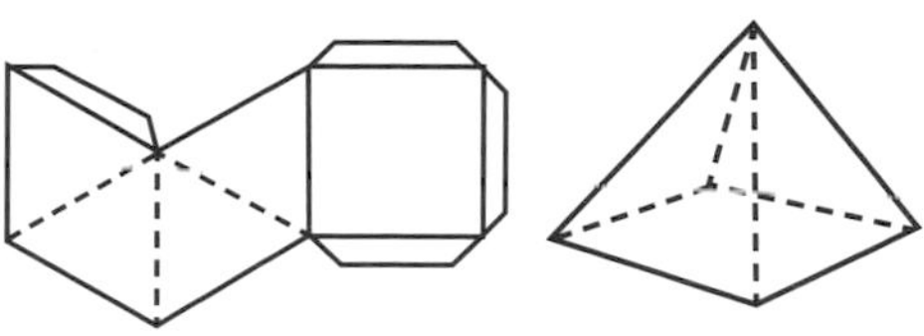

nonagon

A 2-D shape (polygon) with nine sides and nine angles.

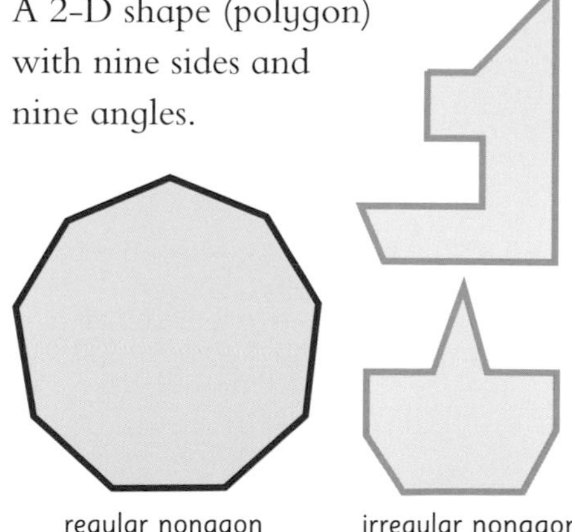

See **polygon**

none

Nothing, not one, not any.

I have 2 apples. I have none.

See **zero**

not equal

Symbol ≠

4 ≠ 5

Four is not equal to five.

See **inequality**

nothing

Symbol 0

Not one; having not a thing; not anything.

See **none, zero**

number expander

A folded strip of paper used to learn place value.

number line

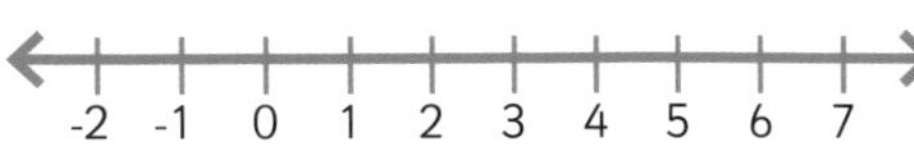

A line on which equally spaced points are marked and numbered. It shows the position of a number. Operations with numbers can be shown on a number line.

Add three and four:

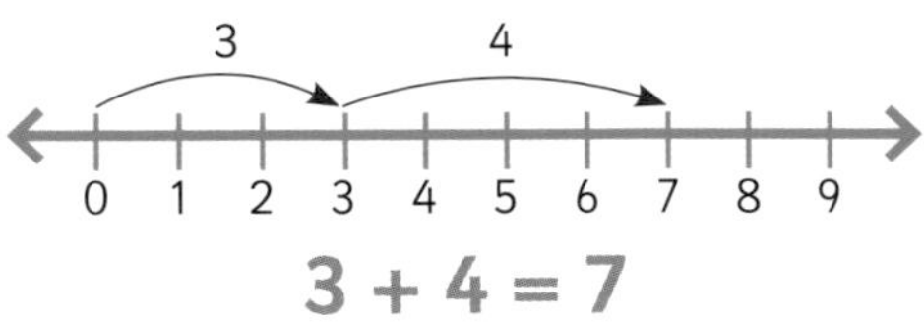

3 + 4 = 7

Subtract five from nine:

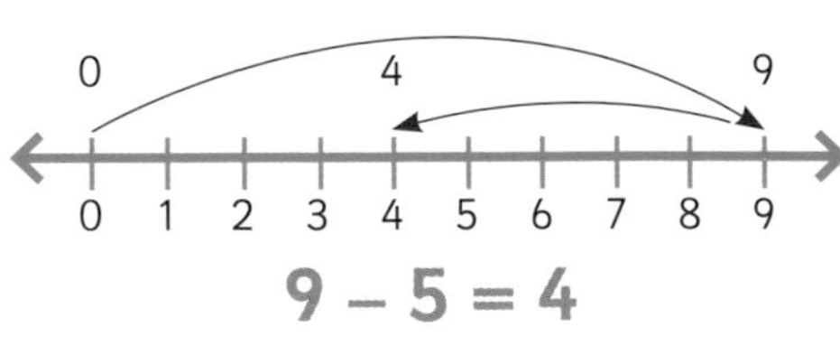

9 – 5 = 4

See **operation**

number

How many things; a measure of quantity. Numbers are grouped into many different sets:

1. Natural (counting) numbers:

1, 2, 3, 4, 5, 6...

2. Whole numbers:

0, 1, 2, 3, 4, 5...

3. Integers:

... -4, -3, -2, -1, 0, +1, +2, +3...

number machine

Number machines can carry out operations such as addition, subtraction, multiplication, and division. Calculators and computers are types of number machines.

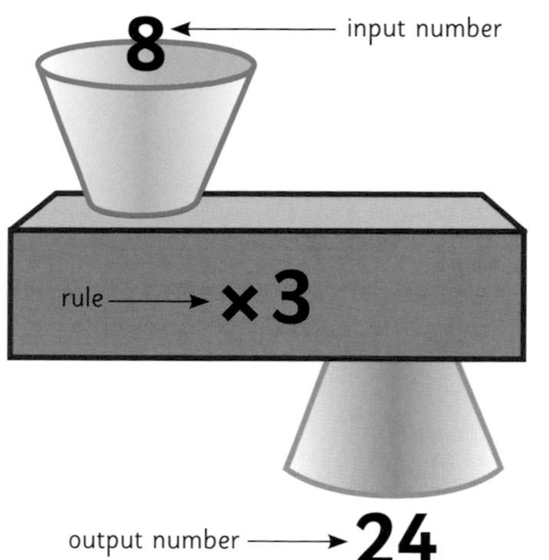

1. The number 8 is put into the machine. This is the input number.
2. The number is multiplied by 3. This is the rule.
3. What comes out of the number machine is the answer.

See **rule**

number pattern

See **pattern**

number sentence

A statement about numbers, usually written in symbols rather than words. A number sentence can be true or false, open or closed.

$6 + 7 = 13$ (true)

$4 \neq 9$ (true)

$5 + ? = 9$ (open)

$7 + 9 = 10$ (false)

$3 + 1 < 3 \times 1$ (false)

$7 - ? = 0$ (open)

See **inequality, open number sentence**

4. Rational numbers, which include fractions and ratios:

5. Other kinds of numbers include complex, composite, prime, odd, even, square, triangular, rectangular numbers, etc.

See **composite number, even number, irrational number, odd number, prime number**

number track

A track, as used in board games, where the sections are numbered.

numerator

The top number in a fraction. It tells how many parts of the whole there are.

$$\frac{3}{4}$$

numerator (3)
denominator (4)

$\frac{3}{4}$ means there are 3 parts out of a possible 4 parts.

See **denominator, fraction**

numeric expression

A number expression without an equals sign. It is also called an arithmetic expression.

4 + 6

numeral

A symbol used to represent a number.

5 is the numeral that represents the number five.

5 apples

V The Roman numeral for the number five is V.

numeration A system of symbols used to represent numbers. Our system uses the symbols:

0, 1, 2, 3, 4, 5, 6, 7, 8, 9

See **Hindu–Arabic, Roman numerals**

oblique

A slanting line.

See **askew**

oblong

Another word for a rectangle.

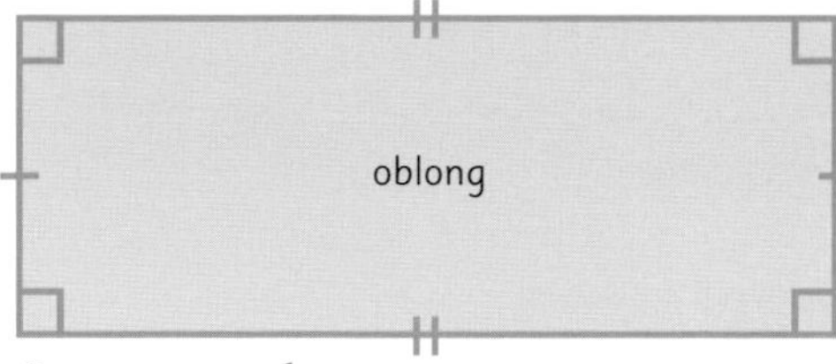

See **rectangle**

obtuse angle

An angle bigger than 90°, but smaller than 180°.

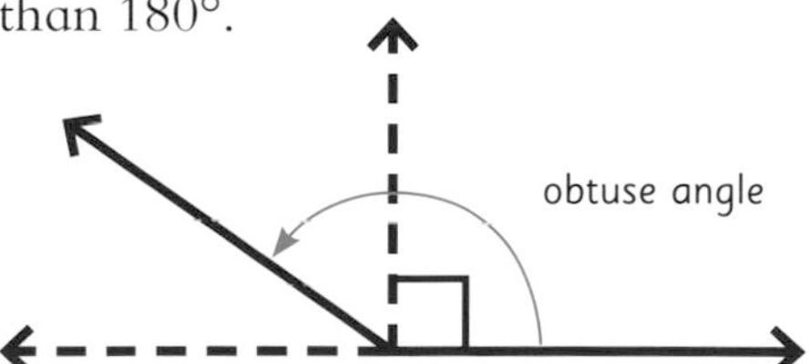

obtuse triangle A triangle with one obtuse angle.

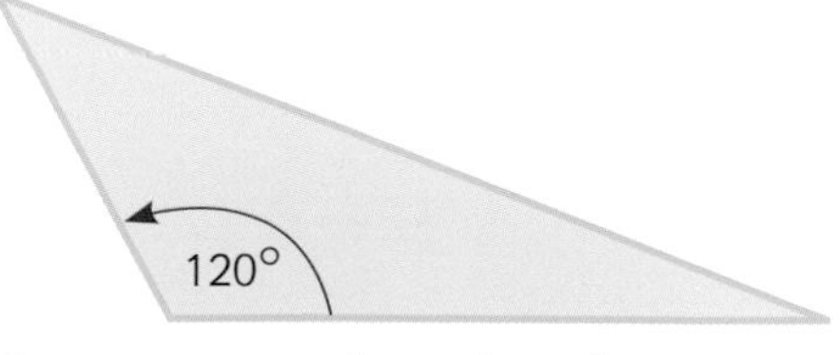

See **acute, angle, triangle**

o'clock

A way of saying "of the clock" when telling the exact hour.

octagon

A 2-D shape (polygon) with 8 straight sides and 8 angles.

regular octagon

irregular octagons

See **plane shape, polygon**

octahedron

A 3-D shape (polyhedron) with 8 faces. A regular octahedron is made of 8 equilateral triangles.

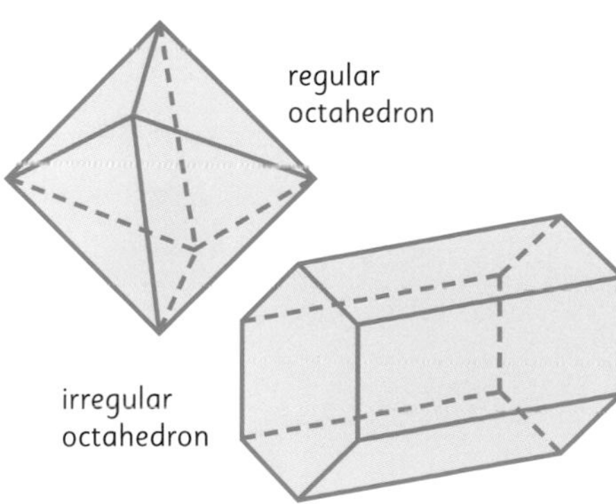

See **polyhedron**

odd number

A number that cannot be divided exactly by 2. Odd numbers finish with 1, 3, 5, 7, or 9.

See **even number**

one-dimensional

A figure that only has length.

1-D figures

A line is one-dimensional.
See **dimension, plane**

one-to-one correspondence

Matching between two sets where each member of one set is paired with one member of the other set.

Cup and saucer

Set A =	Grandpa	Jamil	Dad
	↕	↕	↕
Set B =	tongs	plate	hot dog

See **arrow diagram, mapping, set**

open curve

See **curve**

open number sentence

A mathematical sentence that contains numbers and variables (unknowns). It can be an equation (both parts are equal) or an inequation (parts are not equal).

Equation
$$6 + \Delta = 10$$

Inequation
$$7 + a > 5$$

See **equation, inequality, number sentence, place holder, variable**

operation

There are four arithmetic operations: addition, subtraction, multiplication, and division.
See **addition, arithmetic, basic facts, division, multiplication, subtraction**

operators

The signs used in operations. These include:

$+ \quad - \quad \times \quad \div$

opposite numbers

Two numbers that add up to zero.

$$-5 + 5 = 0$$

The opposite to –5 is 5.

order

To arrange in a pattern or a sequence according to size, value, etc. A pattern or sequence.

Rabbits in order from smallest to largest.

See **ascending order, descending order, pattern, sequence**

ordered pair

An x-coordinate and a y-coordinate written as a pair, with the x-coordinate first.

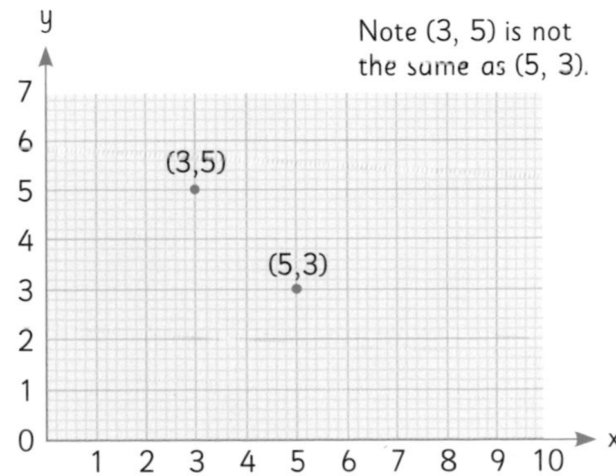

See **coordinates**

order of operations

Used when sorting complicated number sentences.

1. Number sentences with grouping symbols. Working out is done from inside the brackets to the outside.

Example

$$5 + \{10 - (4 \times 2)\}$$
$$= 5 + \{10 - (8)\}$$
$$= 5 + \{2\} = 7$$

2. When there are no grouping symbols, start from the left, insert brackets around multiplication and division, then calculate them. Then start again from the left and first do additions, then subtractions.

Example

$$48 \div 3 + 2 - 4 \times 3$$
$$= (48 \div 3) + 2 - (4 \times 3)$$
$$= 16 + 2 - 12$$
$$= 18 - 12 = 6$$

Note To help remember the order of operations, think BODMAS: Brackets first, Order, Division, Multiplication, Addition, Subtraction.

See **brackets, operation**

ordinal number

A number that indicates position.

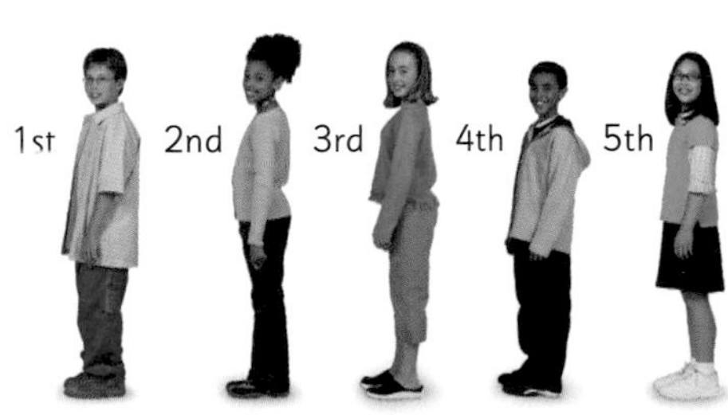

See **cardinal number**

origin

A point at which something begins.

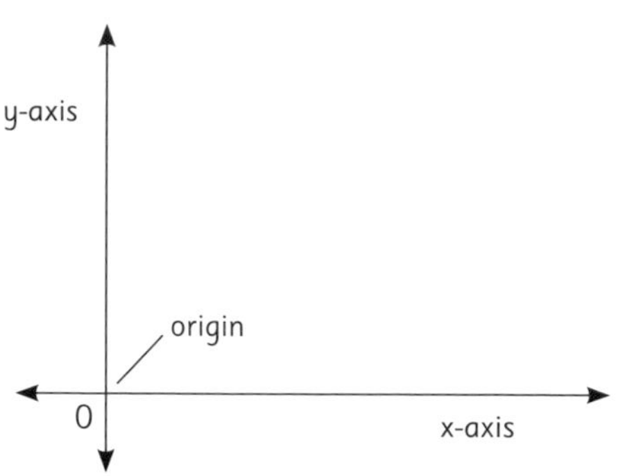

The point where the x and y axes intersect is called the origin and is marked 0. Its coordinates are (0, 0).
See **axis, coordinates, intersect**

ounce

Symbol oz
An imperial unit of weight or mass.
16 oz = 1 pound (lb)

outcome

The result of an experiment where the end result is not known in advance.
Example
There are two possible outcomes of tossing a coin: either heads or tails.
See **event, probability**

output

The number (the answer) that comes out of a number machine after an input number has been put in, and a rule has been applied.
Example
5 is the input number.
The rule is multiply by 3.
The output number is 15.
See **input, number machine**

oval

1. An egg-shaped figure that is symmetrical along one axis. One end is more pointed than the other.

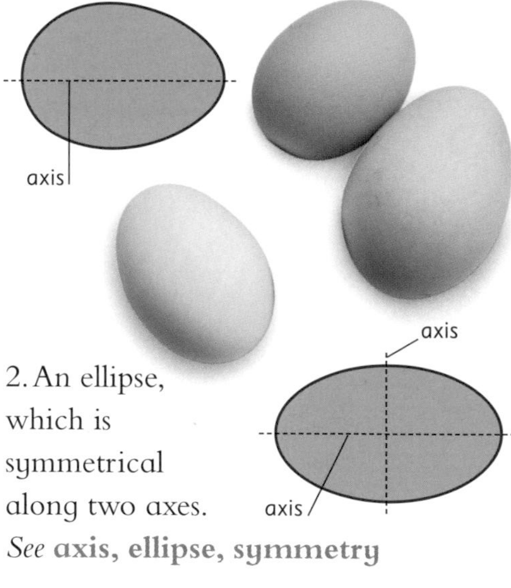

2. An ellipse, which is symmetrical along two axes.
See **axis, ellipse, symmetry**

overdraft

The result of removing more money out of a bank account than you actually have in it.
See **credit, debit**

Pp

pace

The distance between your feet when you take a step, measured from heel to heel. Pace is an arbitrary unit for measuring distances.

Example

Jack's pace measures 55 centimetres.

1 pace

See **arbitrary unit, distance, measure**

pair

Two things that belong together.

a pair of socks

palindrome

A number, word, or sentence that reads the same forwards as backwards.

1991   19.9.1991   madam

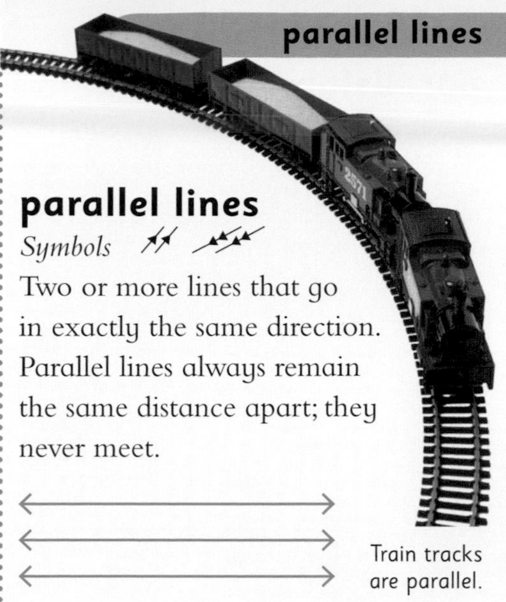

parallel lines

Symbols

Two or more lines that go in exactly the same direction. Parallel lines always remain the same distance apart; they never meet.

Train tracks are parallel.

If parallel lines are crossed by a straight line, pairs of angles are formed:

1. Corresponding angles (they make an F-shape) are equal size.

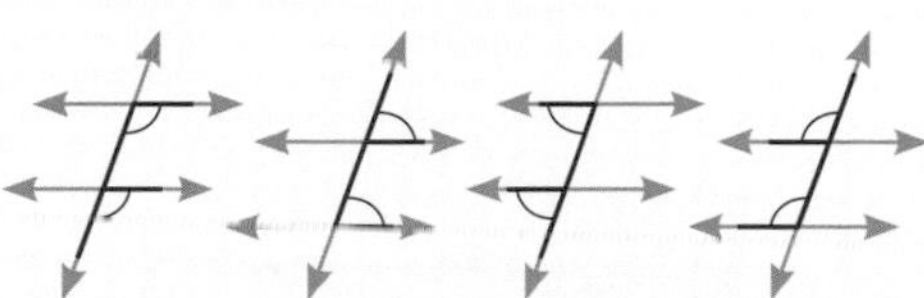

2. Alternate angles (they make a Z-shape) are equal size.

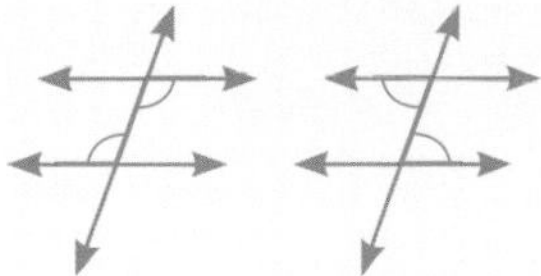

3. Cointerior angles (they make a U-shape) add up to 180°.

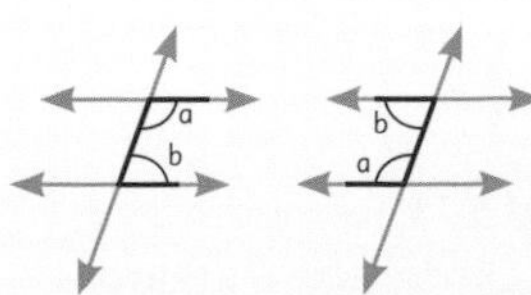

See **vertically opposite angles**

parallelogram

A four-sided shape(quadrilateral) in which both pairs of opposite sides are parallel and equal, and the opposite angles are equal.

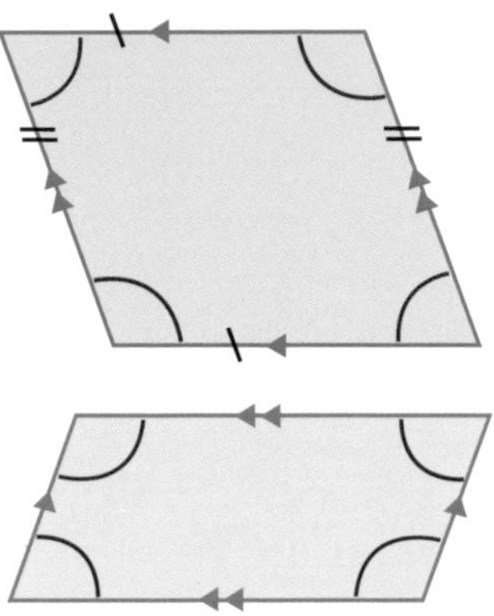

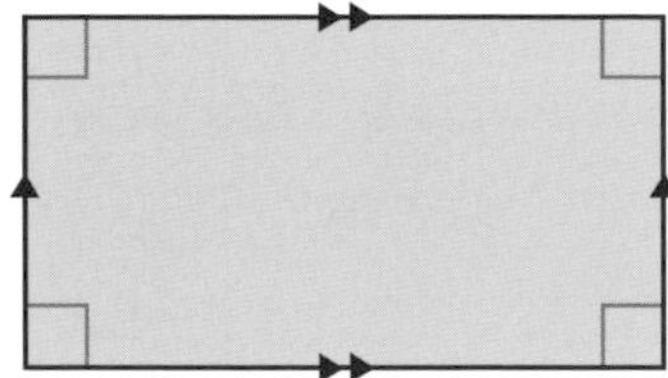

The arrow marks show which pairs of lines are parallel. The marks \ \\ show which lines are of the same length.

A right-angled parallelogram is a rectangle.

See **parallel lines, quadrilateral, rectangle**

parentheses

Another name for curved brackets. ( )

partition

Another name for sharing.

See **division**

Pascal's triangle

An arrangement of numbers used in probability. After the second line down, each number in the triangle is made by adding together the two numbers directly above it.

pattern

A repeated design or arrangement using shapes, colours, numbers, etc.

1. Shape pattern

2. A number pattern is a sequence of numbers formed by following a rule.

1, 4, 7, 10... (rule: add three)

See **rule, sequence**

penny

Plural pennies

A coin equal to one-hundredth of a dollar. The plural is pennies, but when referring to a sum of money, you might say cents.

pentagon

A 2-D shape (polygon) with five straight sides and five angles.

regular pentagon

irregular pentagon

See **polygon**

percent (percentage)

Symbol %

A number out of one hundred.

40% of the bowling pins have been knocked over.

This is a "hundred square". Fifteen out of the hundred little squares have been coloured in dark orange.

They represent:

$$\frac{15}{100} = 0.15 = 15\%$$

fraction — decimal fraction — percentage

See **decimal fraction, fraction**

perimeter

The distance around a closed figure, or the length of its boundary.

To find the perimeter of a figure, add the lengths of all its sides.

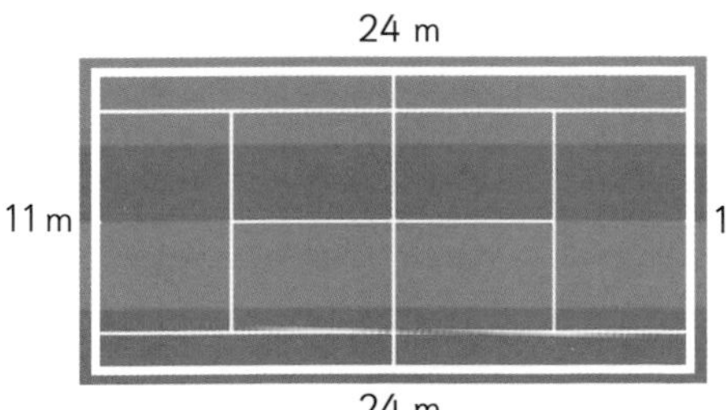

The perimeter of a tennis court is:

24 m + 11 m + 24 m + 11 m = 70 m

See **boundary**

permutation

An ordered arrangement or sequence of a group of objects.

Example

Three shapes can be arranged in six different ways, so they have six permutations:

The order in which the shapes are arranged is important in a permutation. When the order is not important, the arrangement is called a combination.

See **combination**

perpendicular

Forming a right angle.

perpendicular height A line drawn from the top (vertex) of a figure to the base opposite at a 90° angle.

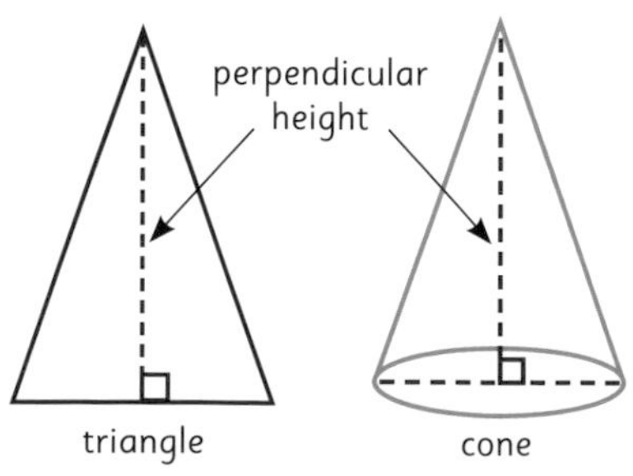

perpendicular lines Lines that meet or intersect to make right angles.

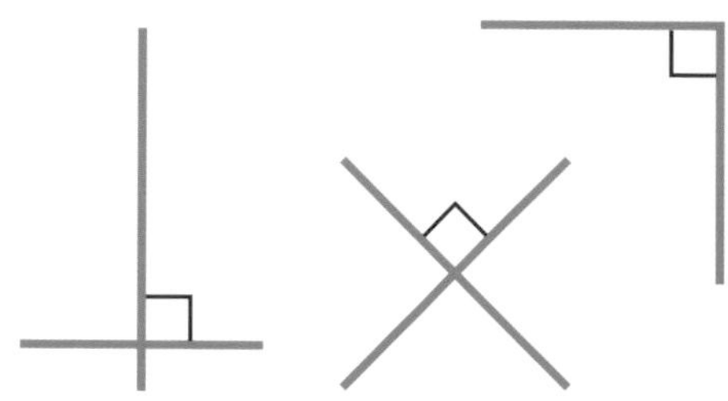

See **apex, cone, line, triangle, vertex**

perspective

When drawing, we can show depth by running all parallel lines to one or several points on the horizon. These points are called vanishing points. This makes a two-dimensional drawing look three-dimensional. We say it has perspective.

See **converging lines, horizon, three-dimensional, two-dimensional**

pi

Symbol π

The number you get when you divide a circle's circumference by its diameter.

$$\pi = \frac{\text{circumference}}{\text{diameter}}$$

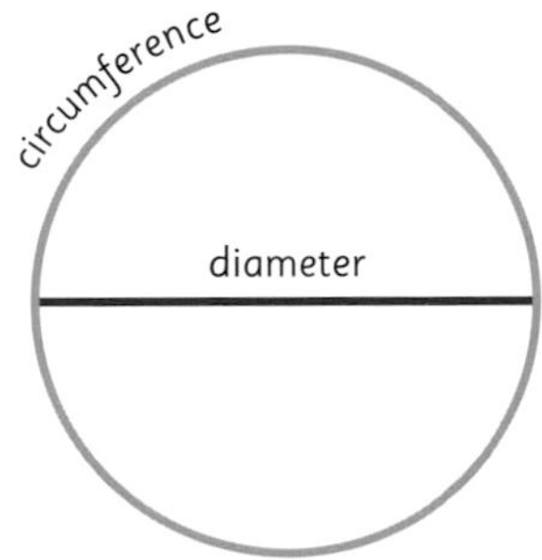

The approximate value of π is 3.14. It is an infinite (endless) decimal. The exact value cannot be worked out.

See **circle, diameter, infinite, radius, ratio**

pictograph

pictogram, picture graph

See **graph**

pie graph

See **graph**

pint

Symbol pt

An imperial unit used to measure the capacity of liquids.

8 pints = 1 gallon

1 pint = approximately 0.5 litres

place holder

1. A symbol that holds the place for an unknown number.

In $w + 3 = 7$, w is the place holder.

In ★ – 6 = 10, ★ is the place holder.

2. Zero, when used with other digits, is used as a place holder. This is called the identity element in addition.

6800

The zeros shows us that the 6 means six thousands, the 8 means eight hundreds, and that there are no tens and no units.

See **digit, equation, variable**

place value

The value of each part of a number depends on its place or position in that number.

hundreds	tens	units
4	8	6

In the number 486, 6 means six units (ones), 8 means eight tens, and 4 means four hundreds.

See **decimal place-value system, digit, value**

plan

1. To prepare ahead of time.
Example Plan for a holiday.
2. A diagram of an object as seen from above.

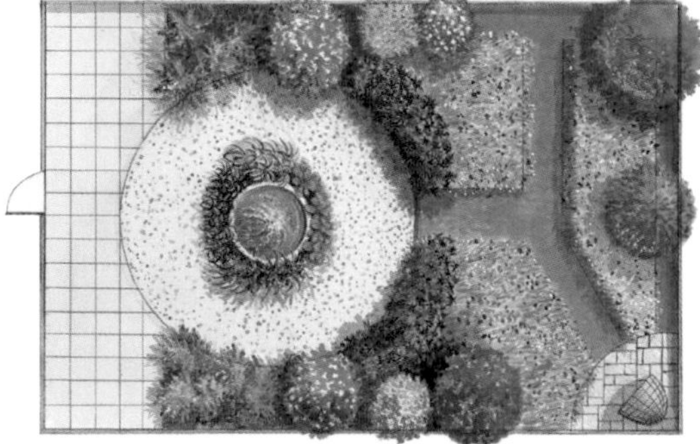

garden plan

See **cross section of a solid, diagram, front view, side view**

plane

A flat surface, such as the floor of a house or a wall. A plane extends infinitely in all directions.

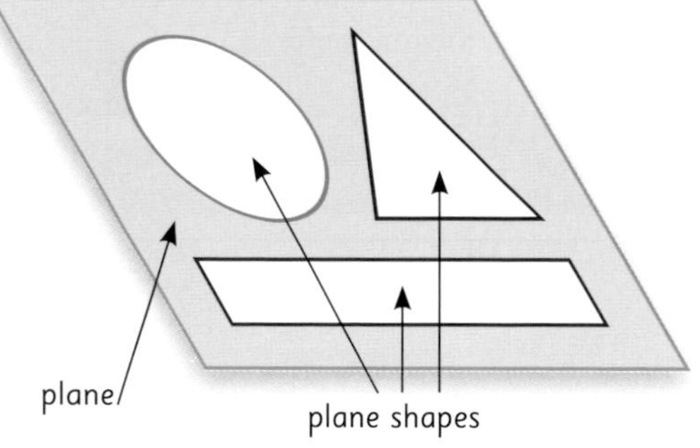

plane shape A closed figure that can be drawn on a flat surface. All two-dimensional objects are plane shapes (planar figures), because they can be drawn in one plane.

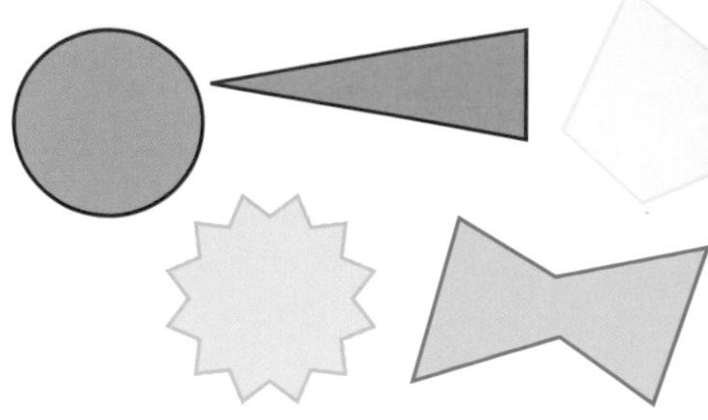

See **dimension, infinite, polygon, two-dimensional**

plus

Symbol +

The name of the symbol that represents addition.

4 + 6 = 10

See **addition**

p.m. (post meridiem)

See **time**

point

1. A small dot on a surface, which has no dimension.

.P

The dot shows where the point P is.

2. In money, a point separates the units of currency (such as dollars) from the parts of the units (cents).

$4.50

The point shows 4 = four dollars and 50 = fifty cents.

See **decimal point, penny, pound**

polygon

A 2-D (plane) shape that has three or more straight sides.

regular polygon A polygon with equal sides and angles.

irregular polygon A polygon where the sides and angles are not all equal.

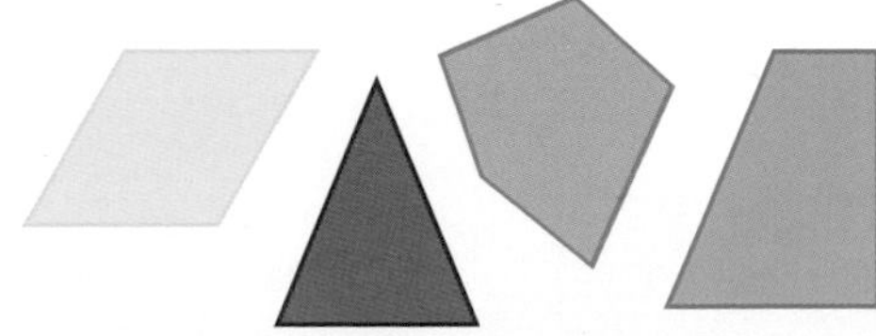

See **angle, closed figure, hexagon, pentagon, plane shape, quadrilateral, side, triangle, two-dimensional**

polyhedron

Plural polyhedrons or polyhedra

A 3-D shape with flat (plane) faces.

regular polyhedron

All faces are regular polygons and all are the same size.

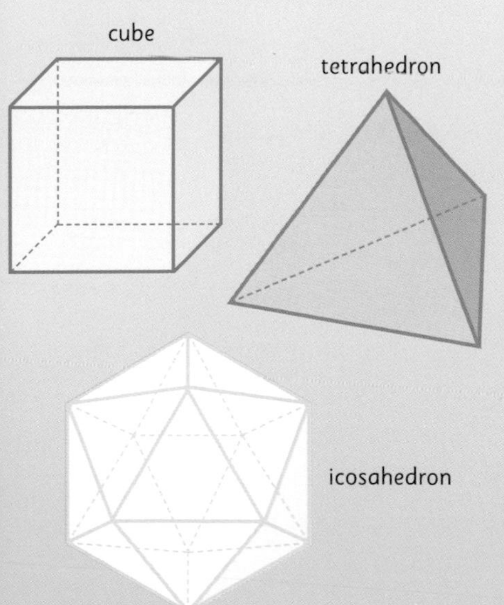

irregular polyhedron

Faces are different sizes and angles and are not all equal.

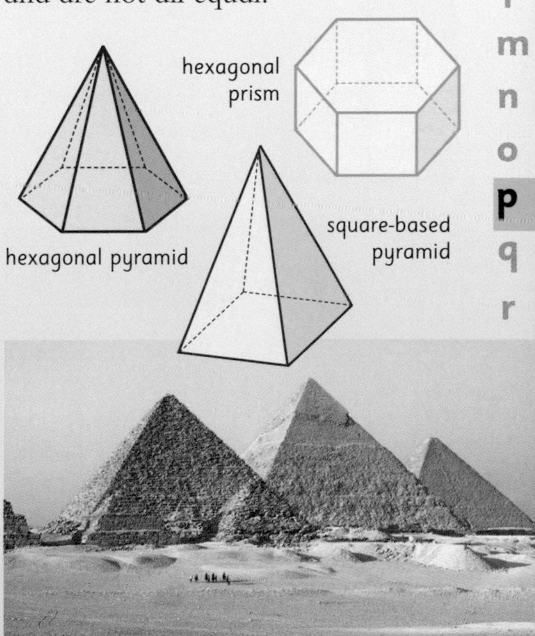

The pyramids of Egypt are square-based pyramids.

See **cube, icosahedron, prism, pyramid, tetrahedron**

a b c d e f g h i j k l m n o p q r y z

polyomino

A plane shape made of squares of the same size, with each square connected to at least one of the others by a common edge.

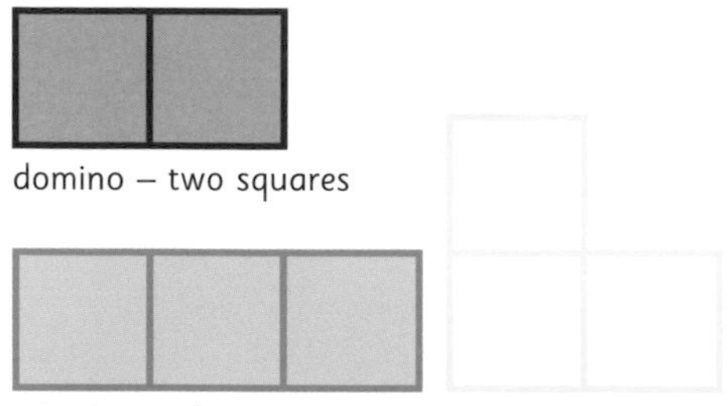
domino – two squares

triomino – three squares

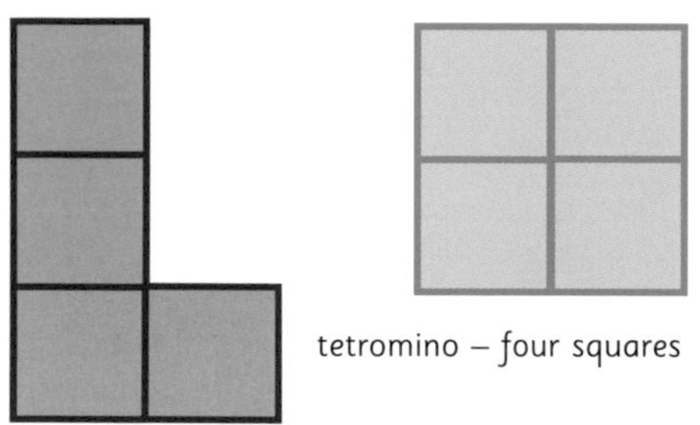
tetromino – four squares

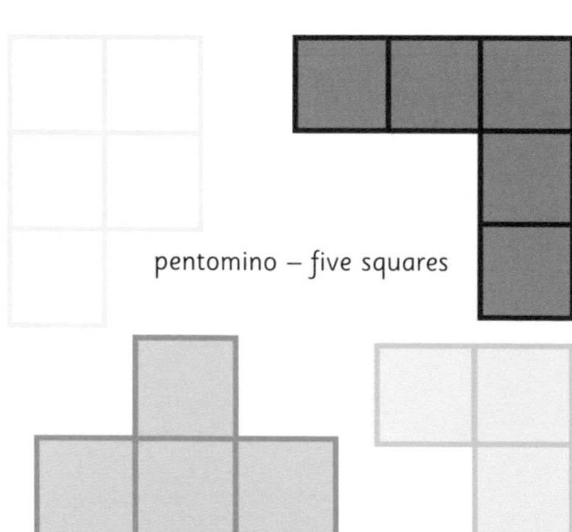
pentomino – five squares

See **plane, two-dimensional**

position

The place where something is.
On, under, above, behind, in front of, between, next to, and outside all describe the position of something.

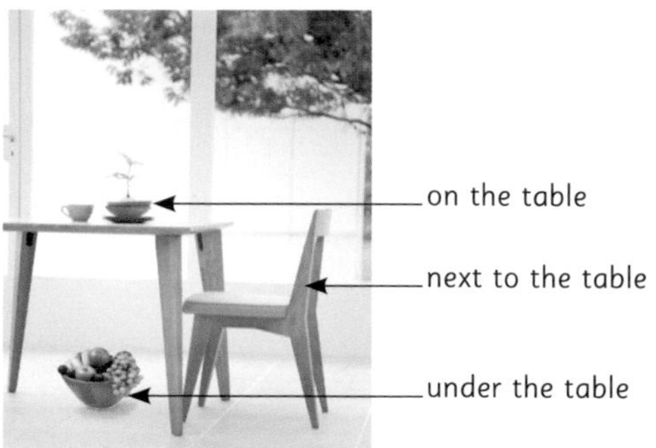

See **coordinates**

positive numbers

Numbers greater than zero.
We sometimes write the plus sign (+) in front of them.

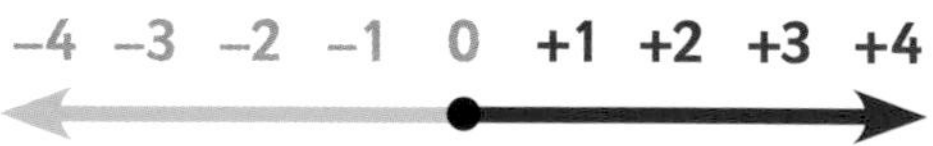

See **integers, negative numbers, plus, zero**

pound

1. *Symbol* £
A unit of money used in the UK. 1£ is worth approximately $2.
2. *Symbol* lb
An imperial unit of weight equal to 16 ounces. 1 lb is approximately 450 grams.
See **ounce**

power (of a number)

The power of a number (also called the index or exponent) shows how many times a number is multiplied by itself.
The power of 2^4 is 4.
It means 2 x 2 x 2 x 2 = 16.
You say "two to the power of four".
When the power is zero, the value is one. $10^0 = 1$ $1000^0 = 1$
See **cubed number, index, square of a number**

prediction

An estimate. In mathematics we may predict, or estimate, possible answers.

prefix

A word added to the start of a unit that tells us how large a measure is.
Kilogram means one thousand grams.

prime factor

A prime number that divides exactly into a given number.
2, 3, and 5 are the prime factors of 30. (10 is also a factor of 30, but not a prime factor.)

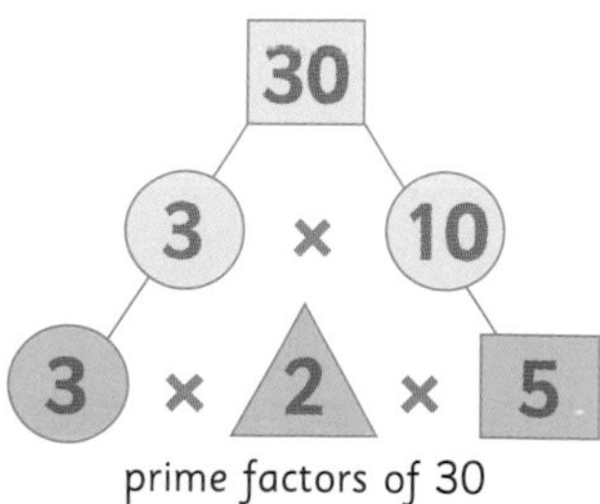

prime factors of 30

product of its prime factors
Finding all the prime numbers that must be multiplied together to get the original number.
1. 12 is divisible by 2, 3, 4, and 6.
2. Only 2 and 3 are prime numbers.
3. Writing 12 as a product of its prime factors reads:
2 x 2 x 3 = 12
See **division, factors, factor tree, inverse, multiplication, prime number, product**

prime number

A counting number that can only be divided by one and itself.

2, 3, 5, 7, 11, 13, 17...

The factors (numbers that divide into another number without leaving a remainder) of two are 2 and 1.
The factors of five are 5 and 1.
Note 1 is not a prime number.
The largest prime number found so far has 12 978 189 digits!
See **composite number, counting number, factors**

principal

The amount borrowed or invested is called the principal.
Example Joe borrowed $100 from a bank. The principal is $100.

prism

A 3-D shape with two parallel faces that are polygons, and the same in shape and size.

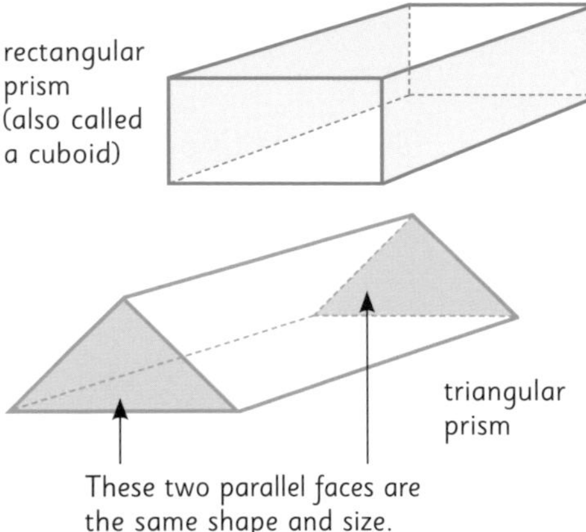

All cuboids are prisms.
See **cuboid, face, parallel lines, polygon, polyhedron, three-dimensional**

probability

The likelihood, or chance of an event happening. There are different types of chance: likely, unlikely, equally likely, impossible, or certain.

1, 2, 3, 4, 5, and 6 are equally likely when you throw a die.

See **certain, chance, event**

problem solving

Using mathematical ideas to find solutions in new situations.
trial and error Selecting a possible answer to a problem, then trying it out to see if it works. If it does not work, another way must be tried.
work backwards When you start with the end result and go backwards, doing the opposite operation for each step.
See **operation**

product

The answer to a multiplication problem.

3 x 2 = 6

multiplicand multiplier product

See **multiplication**

profit

When the selling price is higher than the price the seller paid originally for something, the difference is the profit.

A car dealer buys a car for $20 000. He sells the same car for $22 000. The selling price is $2000 higher than the buying price, so the dealer's profit is $2000.

See **unit price, loss, selling price**

progression

A sequence of numbers following a given rule. The numbers increase or decrease in a constant way.

1. If the rule is "add a number" or "subtract a number" it is called an arithmetic progression.

Rule: add 3

1, 4, 7, 10, 13, 16...

2. If the rule is "multiply by a number" or "divide by a number" it is called a geometric progression.

Rule: multiply by 4

1, 4, 16, 64...

See **decrease, increase, pattern, sequence**

projection

The transformation of one shape or picture to another.

Projecting a picture onto a screen.

See **transformation**

proper fraction

A proper fraction is where the numerator (top number) is less than the denominator (bottom number).

Example

$\frac{4}{5}$ and $\frac{36}{100}$ are proper fractions.

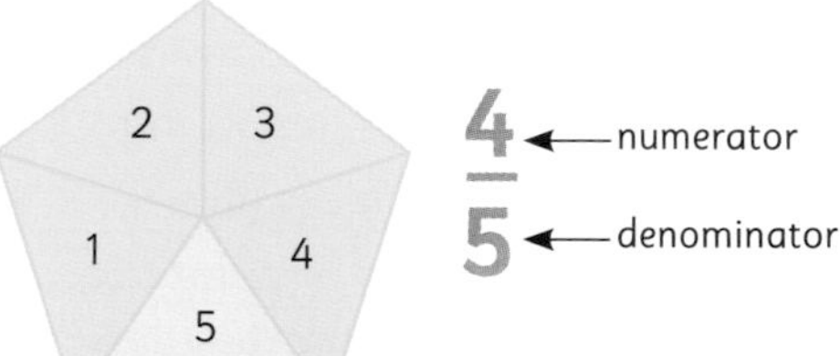

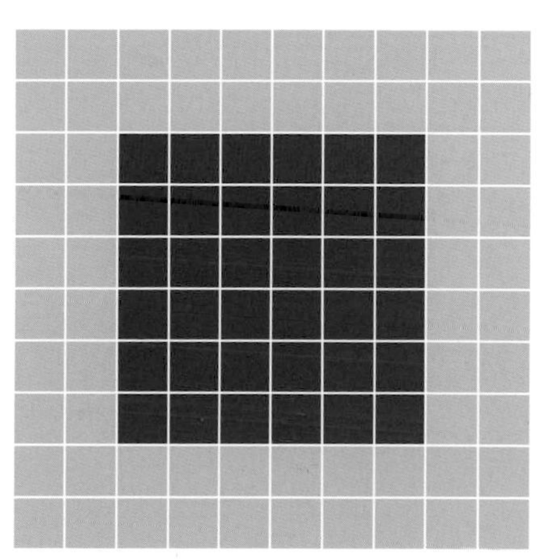

$\frac{36}{100}$ is a proper fraction.

See **denominator, fraction, improper fraction, numerator**

property

A characteristic of an object, such as its length or weight.

See **attribute, classification, proportion**

proportion

Part of a whole, written as a fraction, percentage, or decimal.
Example The drink is $\frac{1}{4}$ (25%, 0.25) juice and $\frac{3}{4}$ (75%, 0.75) water.

direct proportion When two quantities increase or decrease by the same amount, or ratio, the two ratios are equal.

Three cans of paint are enough to paint one wall, so six cans of paint are needed for two walls.

indirect proportion Two quantities are in indirect proportion when as one gets bigger, the other gets smaller by the same ratio.

It takes one person four hours to mow the lawn. This means it will take two people two hours, and four people one hour.

number of people	1	2	4	8	16
time in hours	4	2	1	$\frac{1}{2}$	$\frac{1}{4}$

in proportion Maps are in proportion to the actual ground. The amount the map is scaled down by is written as a ratio, such as 1:50 000. This means that 1 cm on the map is 50 000 cm of the actual ground.
50 000 cm = 500 m = 0.5 km
See **inverse, ratio**

protractor

An instrument used to measure and draw angles.

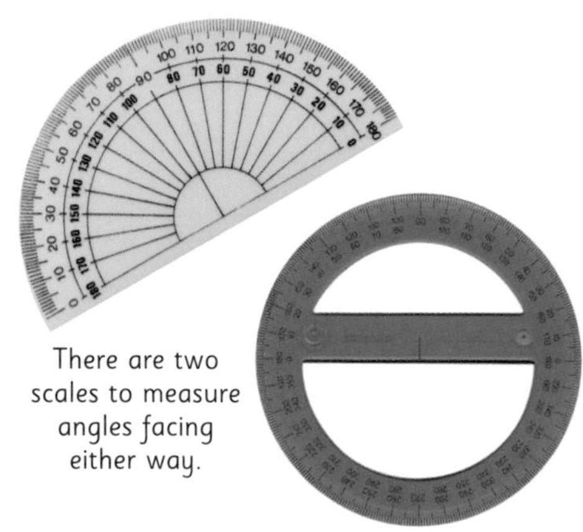

There are two scales to measure angles facing either way.

prove

Test the correctness of a calculation.

pyramid

A 3-D shape that has any type of polygon for a base, and triangular sides.

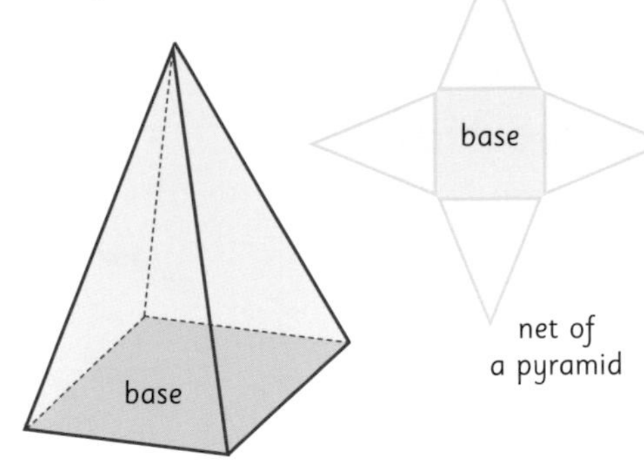

This pyramid has a square base. The other faces are matching (congruent) triangles.
See **base, congruent, face, net, polygon, polyhedron**

Qq

quadrant

1. A quarter of a circle.

quadrant

2. In coordinate geometry, the space between the x-axis and y-axis is called a quadrant. If we extend the x-axis and the y-axis we can see all four quadrants of the number plane. Quadrants are numbered in a counterclockwise direction.

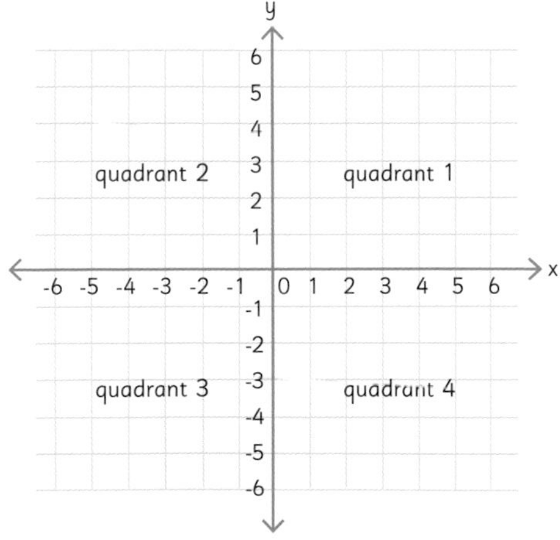

See **circle, coordinates, geometry, ordered pair**

quadrilateral

A 2-D shape (polygon) with four sides and four angles.

Some quadrilaterals are:

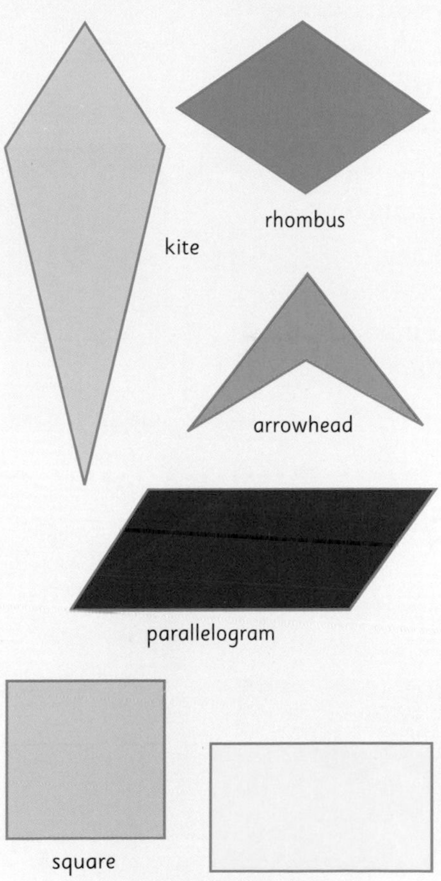

See **kite, parallelogram, rectangle, rhombus, square, trapezium**

quadruple

To increase the amount four times. Quadruple \$20 means:

$$4 \times \$20 = \$80$$

See **double, treble**

quantity

The amount or number of something.

The total quantity of oil in the bottles is 3 litres.

quotient

The answer to a division problem.

$$10 \div 2 = 5$$

dividend ↑ divisor ↑ quotient ↑

Five is the quotient.

See **dividend, division**

quotition

Another name for grouping.

See **division, grouping**

quarter

One of four equal parts.

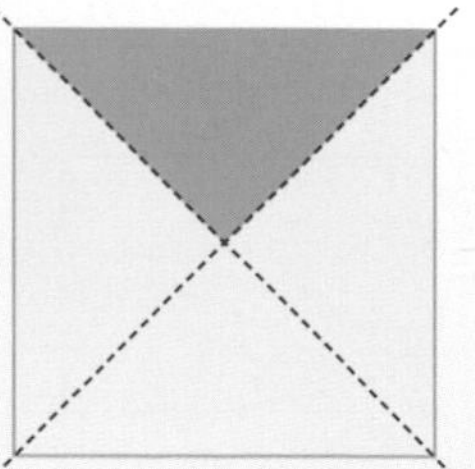

$\frac{1}{4}$ of the square is shaded dark orange.

Each quarter of the pizza has a different topping.

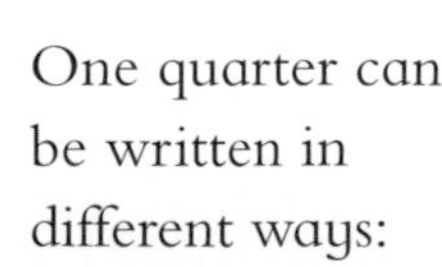

One quarter can be written in different ways:

0.25 decimal

$\frac{1}{4}$ fraction

25% percentage

The orange has been cut into quarters.

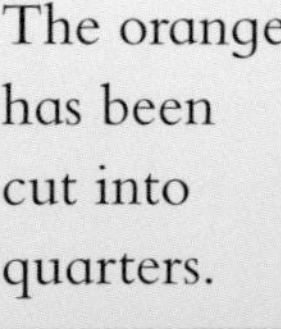

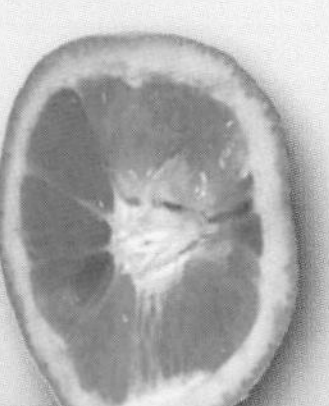

Rr

radius

Plural radii

A straight line that measures the distance from the centre of a circle or sphere to its edge.

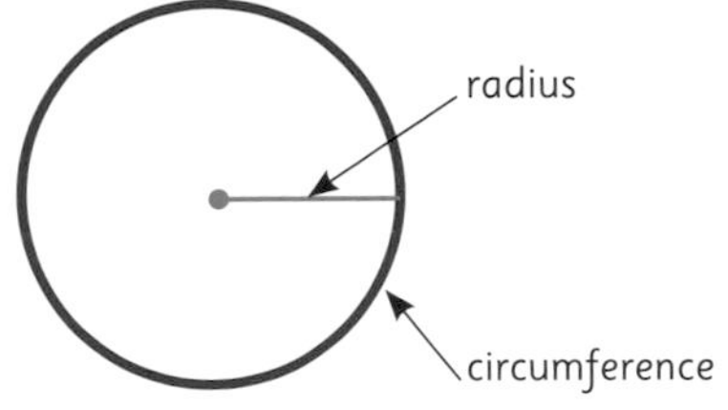

See **centre, circle, diameter, line, sphere**

random sample

A statistics term. A part or portion that is chosen by chance to represent the whole.

range

The difference between the largest and the smallest number in a set.

The smallest number is 2.
The largest number is 8.
8 - 2 = 6.
The range is 6.

rate

When one amount (quantity) is compared to another.

Example

Sixty kilometres per hour (60 km/h) compares kilometres to hours. It indicates the speed of travel.

See **comparison**

ratio

Symbol **:**

A way of comparing amounts (quantities). One quantity is expressed as a part of another.

Example

To make a jug of orange juice, mix 1 part of juice to 3 parts of water. This is a ratio of 1 : 3 (1 is juice and 3 is water).

The order of the numbers is important. In this example, the ratio of juice to water is 1 : 3, not 3 : 1.

See **comparison**

rational number

A number that can be written as a fraction, where the top and bottom of the fraction are whole numbers.

$$0.5 = \frac{1}{2}$$

$$8 = \frac{8}{1}$$

1. It can be represented by decimal numbers that end (terminate).

$$\frac{3}{4} = 0.75$$

2. It can also be represented by numbers that repeat.

$$\frac{2}{3} = 0.6666... \text{ or } 0.\bar{6}$$

See **decimal, fraction, recurring decimal**

ray

A line that has a starting point but no end. It extends in one direction only.

See **line**

real number

The set of real numbers is made up of all rational and irrational numbers. All real numbers are found on the number line.
See **irrational number, number line, rational number**

reciprocal

A fraction made by swapping over the denominator and numerator.
Examples
1. Since we can write 4 as $\frac{4}{1}$, the reciprocal of 4 is $\frac{1}{4}$.
2. The reciprocal of $\frac{2}{3}$ is $\frac{3}{2}$ or $1\frac{1}{2}$.

rectangle

A 2-D, four-sided shape (quadrilateral) with two pairs of equal and parallel sides, and four right angles.

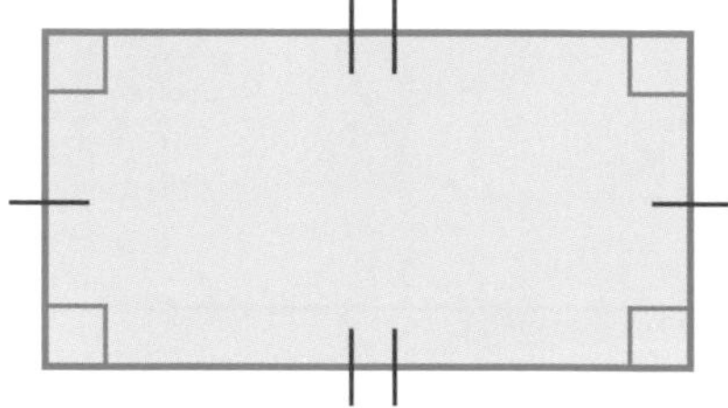

A rectangle is also called an oblong.
See **parallel lines, quadrilateral, right angle**

rectangular number

A number that can be represented by dots arranged in a rectangle.

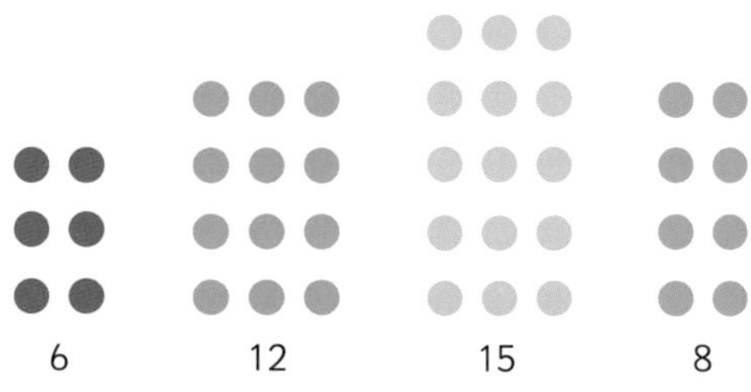

rectangular prism

A 3-D shape (polyhedron) with a rectangular base. Most boxes are rectangular prisms.

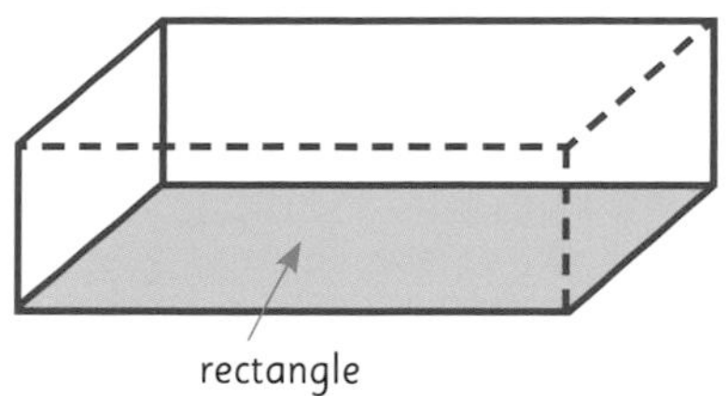

recurring decimal

A decimal with a digit or sequence of digits that repeats indefinitely.

0.6666... or $0.\overline{6}$ ← This bar indicates that the digit repeats.

reduce

To simplify or make smaller. To express a fraction in its simplest form.

Example

$\frac{2}{12}$ can be reduced to $\frac{1}{6}$.

See **cancelling, fraction**

reflection

The mirror image of an object.

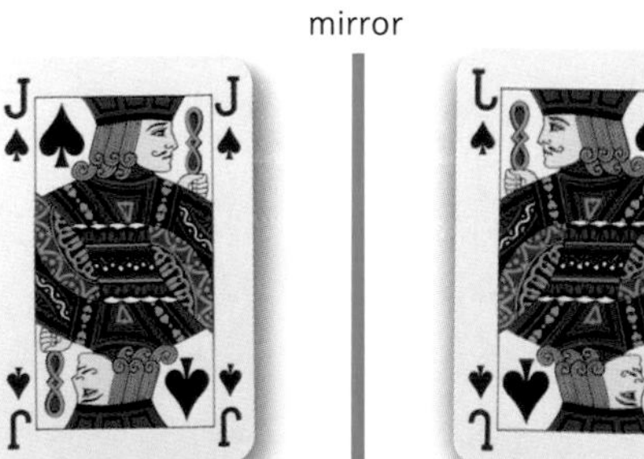

See **flip, mirror image**

reflex angle

An angle greater than a straight angle (180°).

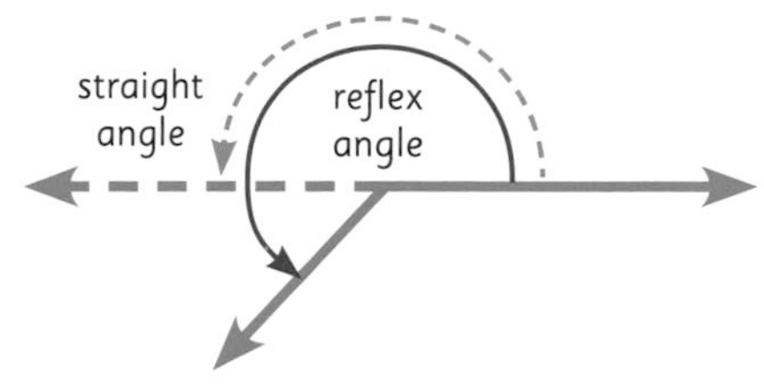

See **angle, revolution, straight angle**

region

plane region All the points inside a closed shape together with all the points on the edge of the shape.

solid region All the points inside a closed area together with all the points on the surface.

Examples

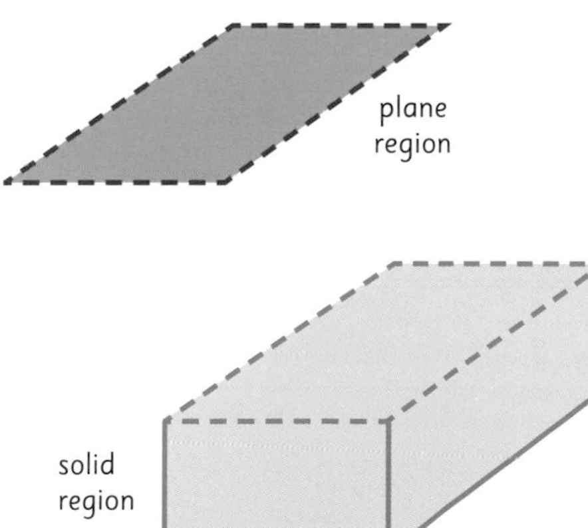

See **boundary, plane, solid, surface**

regroup

Exchange.

Example

Twelve unit blocks can be regrouped (exchanged) into 1 long block (a group of 10 units) and 2 units.

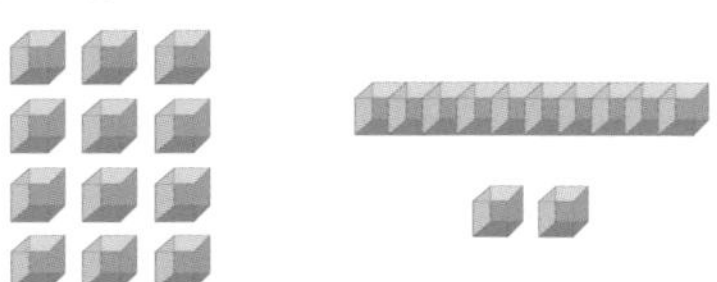

See **base ten blocks, exchange, group**

regular shape

See **polygon**

relation

relationship

The connection between a pair of objects, measures, numbers, etc.

The relation between pairs of numbers can be shown as an equation. The relation between the two rows in this table is $y = x + 5$.

x	1	2	3	4	5
y	6	7	8	9	10

remainder

The amount left over when a number does not divide exactly into another number.

$7 \div 2 =$ can be written as $2\overline{)7}$

2 can go into 6 exactly three times, but not 7, so we write 3 above the 7.

Then we take 6 away from 7 to find out the remainder.

$$\begin{array}{r} 3 \\ 2\overline{)7} \\ \underline{6} \\ 1 \end{array}$$

There are different ways of writing the remainder in the answer.

1. *Question:* Five boys share 128 marbles. How many marbles does each boy get? *Answer:* Each boy gets 25 marbles. Three marbles are left over.

2. *Question*: Share \$128 between five girls. *Answer:* Each girl gets \$25 and $\frac{3}{5}$ of a dollar, that is \$25 and 60¢.

repeating decimal

See **recurring decimal**

reverse

The opposite way round.

Example

The reverse of A B C is C B A

reverse operation

The opposite of an operation.

Example

Addition is the reverse of subtraction.

See **inverse**

revolution

One complete turn. There are 360° and four right angles in one revolution.

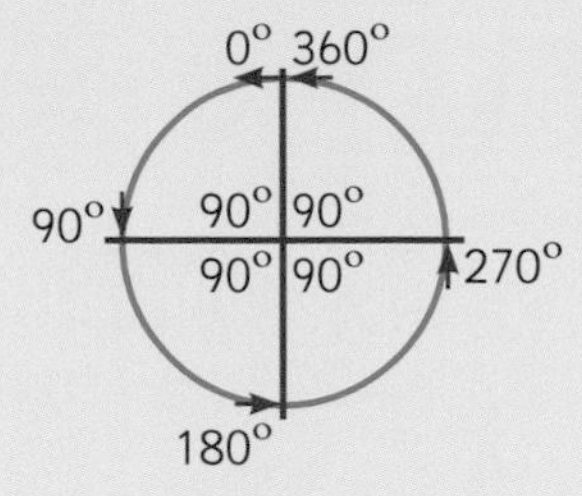

See **angle, right angle**

rhombus

A parallelogram with four equal sides and two pairs of equal angles.

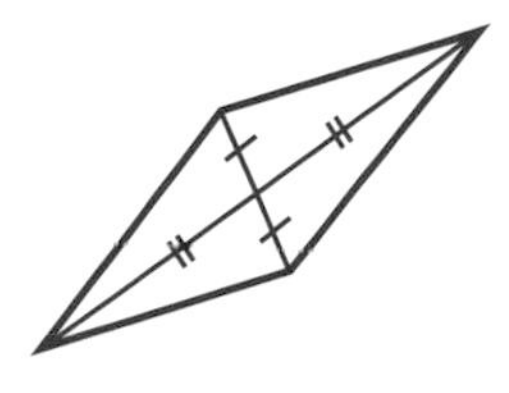

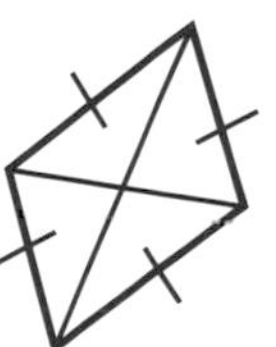

See **diamond, parallelogram**

Roman numerals

The Roman system of numbering where numbers are represented by letters.

I = 1, V = 5, X = 10, L = 50, C = 100
D = 500, M = 1000.

Examples

2000 = MM
2002 = MMII

rotation

rotate

A turning movement around a fixed point.

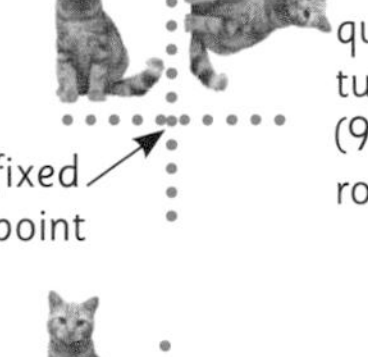

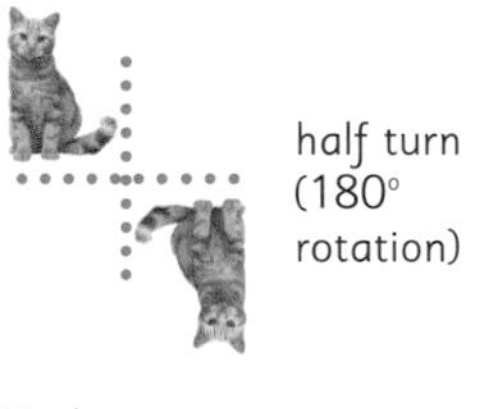

right angle

Symbol ∟

An angle measuring exactly 90°.

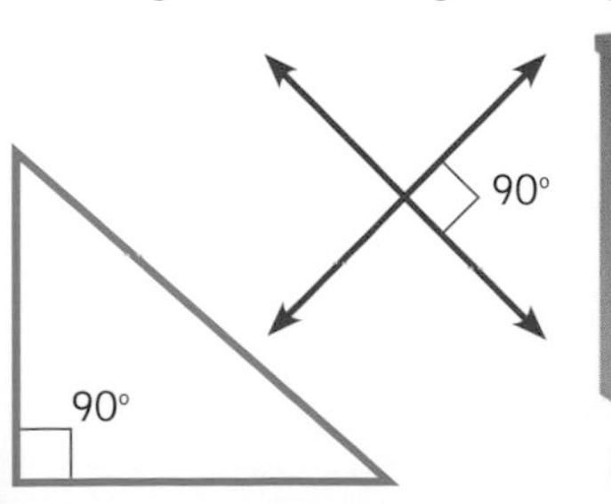

right-angled triangle
A triangle with a right angle.

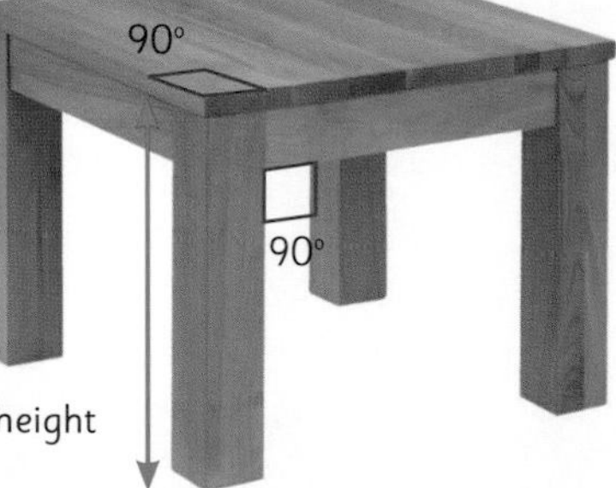

right 3-D shape A solid with an end or base that is 90° to its height, such as a right cone.

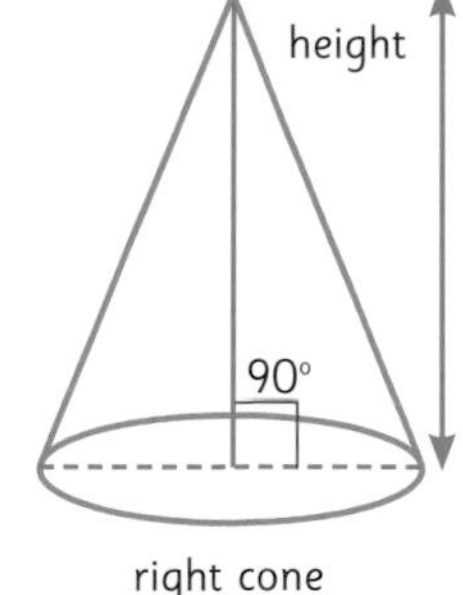

See **angle, cone**

rotational symmetry

A shape has rotational symmetry if it can fit into its outline at least once when it is turned a complete turn (rotation) around a central point.

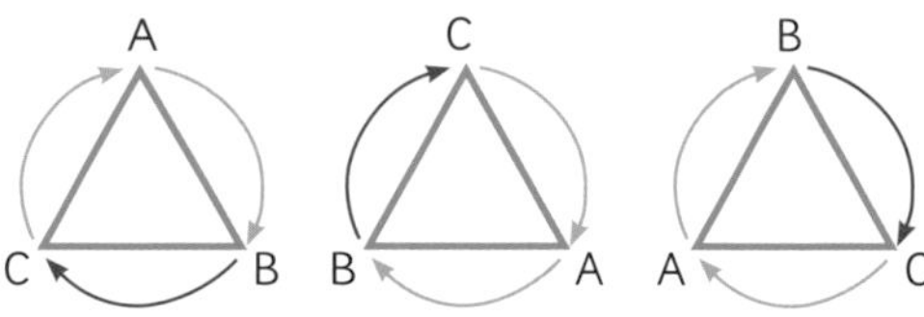

An equilateral triangle has rotational symmetry.

rounding

Writing a number as an approximation by replacing it with the nearest significant figure (usually one that can be divided by 10) to make it easier to work with.

Example

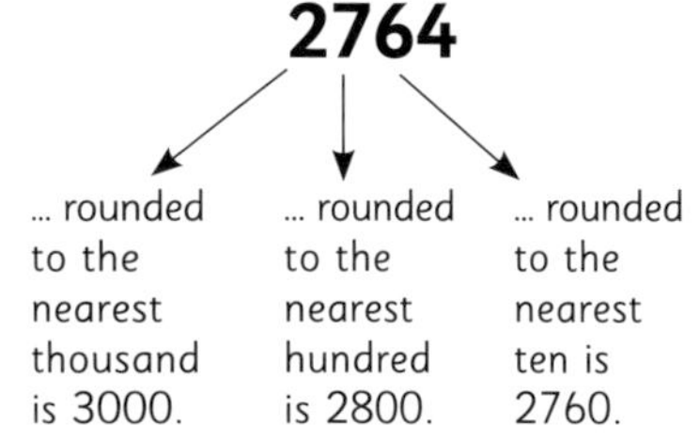

Rounding down

Numbers ending in 1, 2, 3, and 4 round down to the lower significant number: 54 rounded down is 50.

Rounding up

Numbers ending in 5, 6, 7, 8, and 9 round up to the higher significant number: 55 rounded up is 60.

See **accurate, estimate, significant figure**

route

A path or direction leading from one place to another.

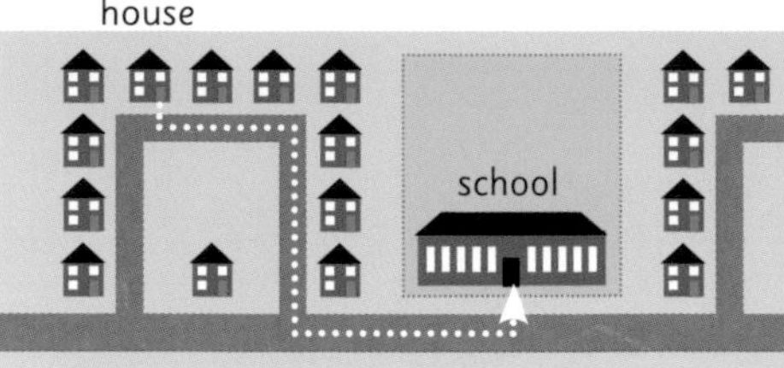

my route to school

row

Things arranged horizontally so that they make a line.

Example A row of numbers:

4, 5, 6, 7, 8, 9...

See **column, horizontal line**

rule

1. An instruction to do something in a particular way.

1 4 7 10 13

+3 +3 +3 +3

The rule for this sequence is "add 3".

2. To draw a line using a ruler.

ruler A device for drawing straight lines and measuring length.

See **graduated, progression**

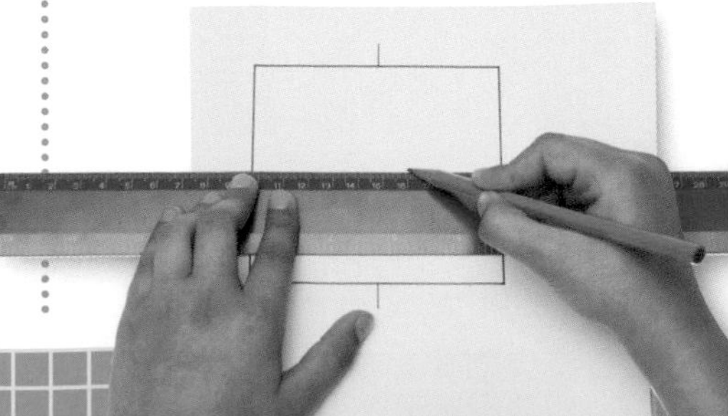

Ss

same

Identical, alike, unchanged, not different.
See **congruent**

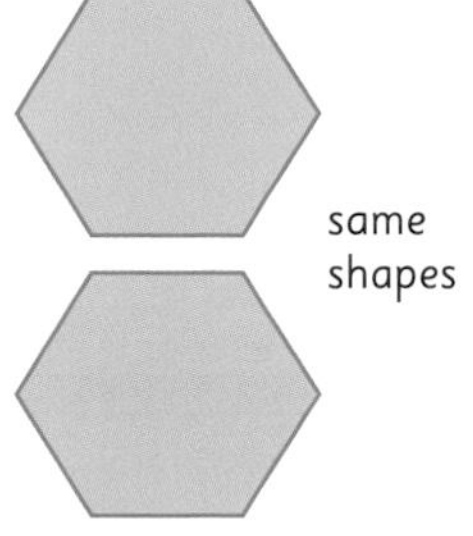

sample

A selection taken from a larger group so that you can find out something about the larger group.

Example

A sample of children were asked about their favourite foods.

sample space

A term used in probability. It shows all the possible results (outcomes) of an experiment. There may be a small or a large number of possible sample spaces.

Activity	Sample space
Rolling a die	{1, 2, 3, 4, 5, 6}
Tossing a coin	{Heads, tails}

See **probability**

scale

1. Equally spaced markings on a measuring device. A thermometer, a ruler, and a balance each have a scale marked on them to measure temperature, length, and mass.

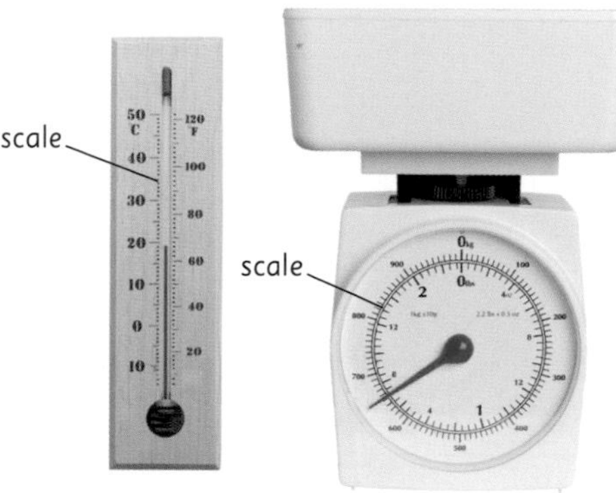

2. A number line used on a graph.

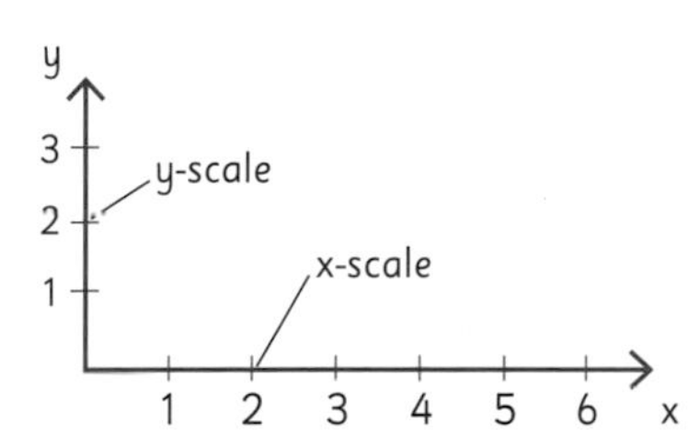

3. The scale on a map or a plan shows the ratio for making things larger or smaller.

Scale of kilometres

1 cm = 10 km

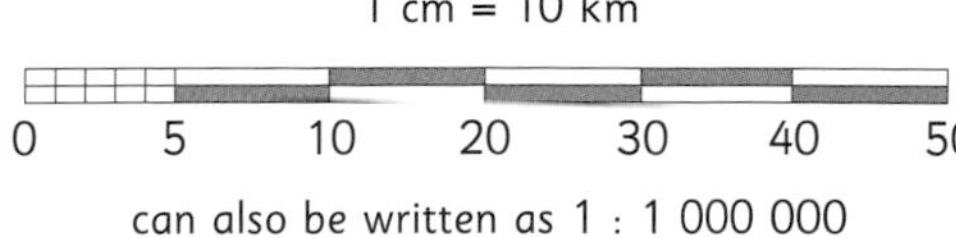

can also be written as 1 : 1 000 000

See **balance, graph, number line, thermometer**

scale drawing

A drawing or plan on which the real object is made bigger or smaller while keeping the same proportions.

The drawing on the right has been scaled down on a scale of 1 to 2 or 1 : 2.

See **proportion, ratio**

scalene triangle

A triangle that has sides of different lengths and three different angles.

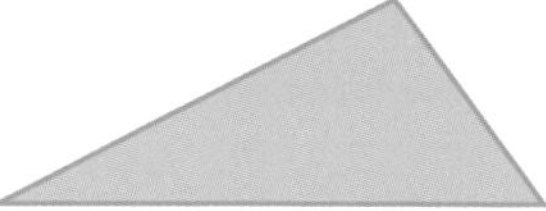

See **triangle**

scales

Instruments used for finding or comparing weights or masses.

bathroom scales

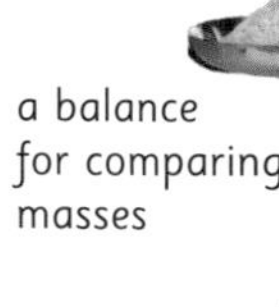

a balance for comparing masses

See **balance, mass, spring balance, weight**

scatter plot

A graph of plotted points that shows a relationship between two sets of information (data), one along the x-axis and one along the y-axis. Also called a scatter diagram.

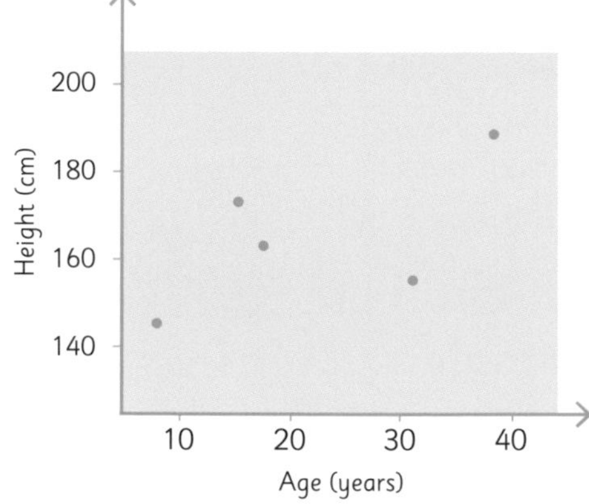

A scatter plot comparing the height versus age in a family of five.

scientific notation

A quick and easy way of writing very big or very small numbers using powers of ten.

$$10\ 352 = 1.0352 \times 10^4$$

This tells us that the decimal point must move four places to the right.

$$1\ 300\ 000 = 1.3 \times 10^6$$

This tells us that the decimal point must move six places to the right.

See **power (of a number)**

score

The amount of points or marks gained in a competition or test.

	TEST				
1	6+1=7 ✔		6	5+5=10 ✔	
2	3+3=6 ✔		7	3+1=5 ✘	
3	5-2=3 ✔		8	3+7=10 ✔	
4	10-2=7 ✘		9	1+8=9 ✔	
5	10-7=3 ✔		10	4+4=8 ✔	
				Score = 8/10	

second

The ordinal number (one that indicates position) that comes after first (1st).

See **ordinal number**

second

See **time**

section

1. A flat surface obtained by cutting through a solid in any direction.

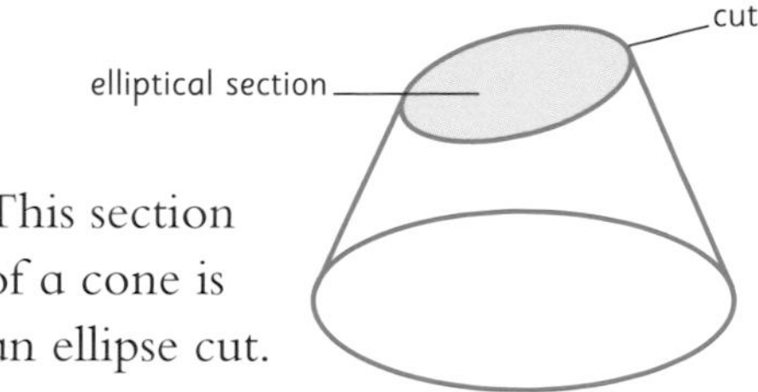

This section of a cone is an ellipse cut.

2. When the cut is parallel to the base or side of the solid, it is called a cross section.

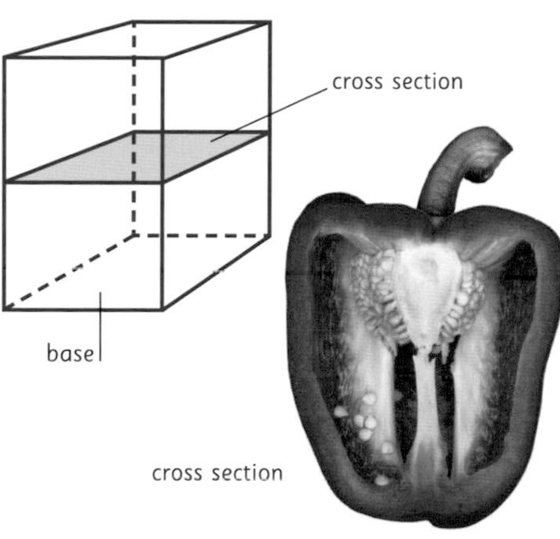

See **cross section of a solid, ellipse, segment, solid, surface**

sector

A part of a circle enclosed by two radii and an arc.

See **arc, circle, radius**

segment

A part, a section of something.
Examples
1. A line segment.

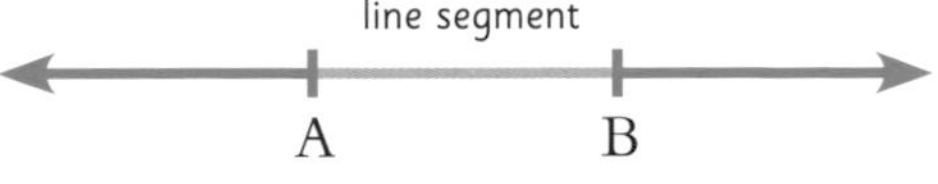

2. A segment of a circle is the part of the circle between an arc and its chord.

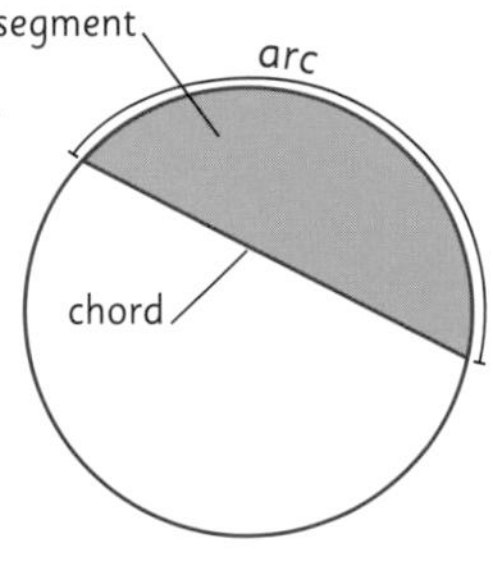

See **arc, circle**

selling price

Price at which something is sold.
Example
A car dealer sells a car for $16 000. The selling price of the car is $16 000.
See **unit price, loss, profit**

semicircle

Half a circle. When you cut a circle along its diameter, you get two semicircles.

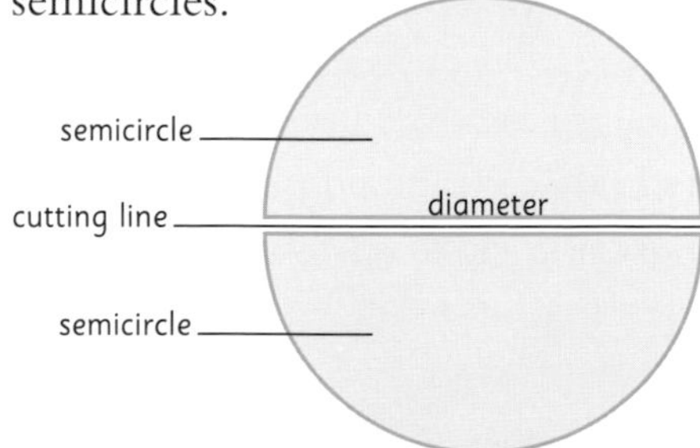

See **circle, diameter**

sentence

A statement. In mathematics a sentence may contain numerals and other symbols.

See **false sentence, number sentence, numeral, open number sentence, true sentence**

sequence

A set of numbers or a pattern following an order or rule.
Examples
1, 3, 5, 7, 9, 11, 13…
The rule of this sequence is "add 2".

In the sequence above, each shape is following a pattern of rotation counterclockwise by the same amount of turn.
See **counterclockwise, order, pattern, progression, rotation, rule**

seriate

To put in order.
Example These sticks are seriated according to length.

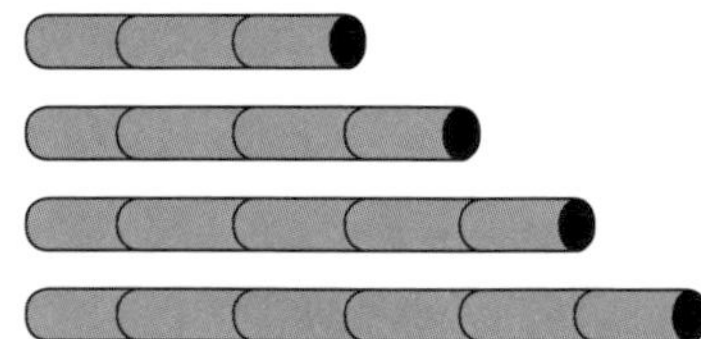

set

Symbol { }

A group of objects or numbers. Each object in a set is called a member or an element of the set. The elements of a set are written inside curly brackets called braces { }.

Example

Set of whole numbers = {0, 1, 2, 3, 4...}

See **element of a set**

set square

An instrument used for geometrical drawings.

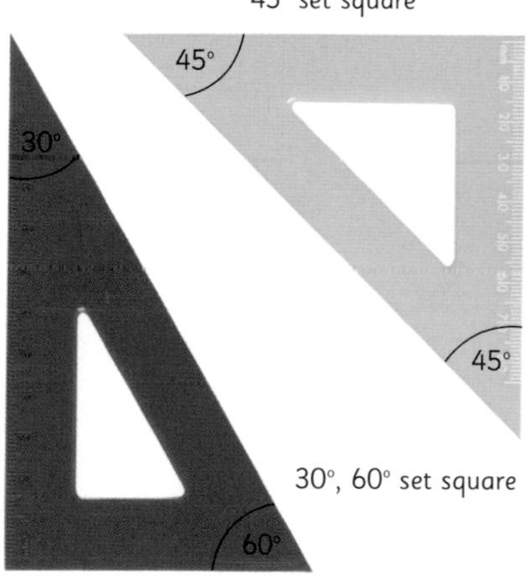

Set squares are used for drawing parallel lines and angles.

See **parallel lines, right angle**

shape

The form of an object. Two-dimensional (2-D) shapes include triangles, quadrilaterals, polygons. Three-dimensional (3-D) shapes include cubes, prisms, and pyramids.

See **cube, dimension, prism, pyramid, quadrilateral, three-dimensional, triangle, two-dimensional**

sharing

See **division**

side

A line segment that is a part of a perimeter or a figure.

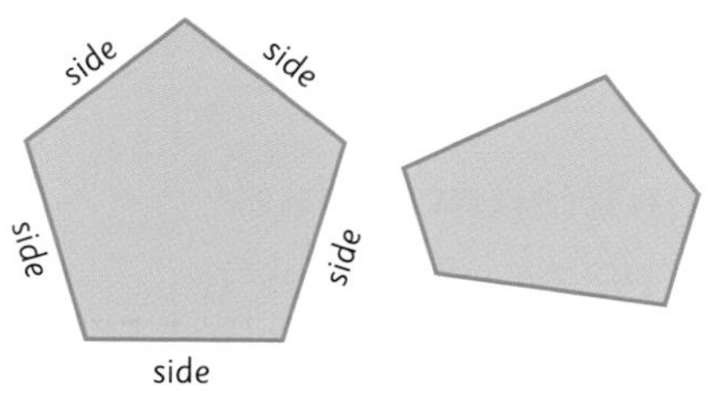

A pentagon has five sides.

See **line segment, pentagon, perimeter**

side view

A diagram, as seen from the side.

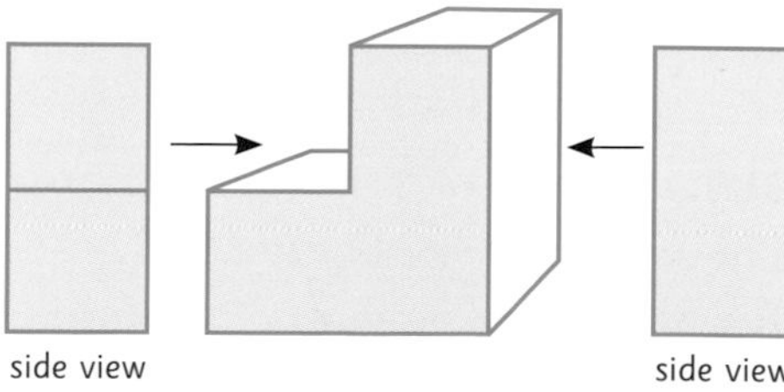

See **cross section of a solid, front view, plan**

sign
A symbol used in math instead of words. Some of the main signs are:

$+$	**Addition**
$-$	**Subtraction**
$\times$	**Multiplication**
$\div$	**Division**
$=$	**Equals**
%	**Percentage**
>	**Greater than**
<	**Less than**

See **operation**

significant figure
A digit in a number that is considered important when rounding numbers up or down or when making an approximation.
Example

3745 rounded to two significant figures is **3700**

0.165m rounded to one significant figure is **0.2m**

See **approximation, rounding**

similar
The same in shape but not in size. Two shapes are similar figures if the corresponding angles are equal and all sides are enlarged or reduced by the same ratio.

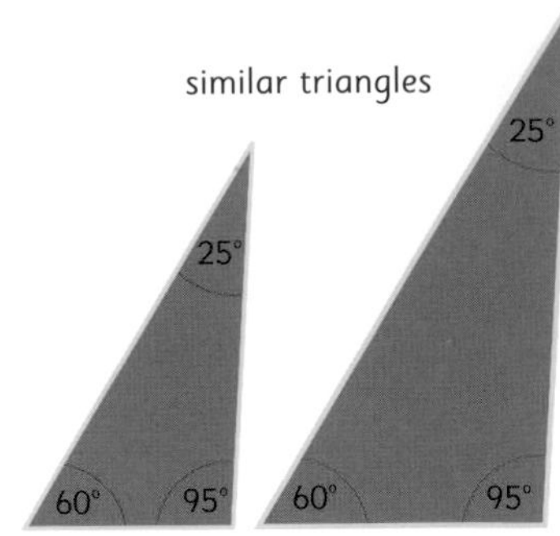

See **congruent, enlarge, ratio, reduce**

simple fraction
See **fraction**

simplify
To write in the simplest, shortest form. These fractions have been simplified by making the numerator and denominator as small as possible.

$$\frac{8}{10} + \frac{4}{20} = \frac{4}{5} + \frac{1}{5} = \frac{5}{5} = 1$$

See **cancelling**

size
The amount or dimensions of something.
The size of this angle is 37°.

37°

skew lines
Lines that do not intersect and are not parallel, so are not on the same plane.
See **intersect, parallel lines**

slide

Change position on the surface.
See **flip, rotation, translation, turn**

slope

The slope of a line measures the steepness, or gradient, of the line. Slope is calculated by dividing the rise by the run.

solid

A solid is a figure with three dimensions, usually length, width, and height.

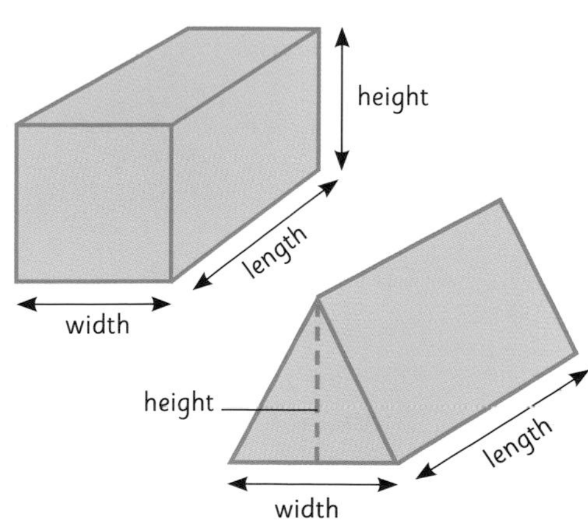

See **height, length, three-dimensional, width**

solution

The answer to a problem or question.
Example

The equation:	$x + 4 = 9$
has a solution:	$x = 5$

solve

Find the answer.
See **calculate, solution**

some

Not all of the whole, a part.

sorting

Putting objects that share similar features (attributes) into groups.

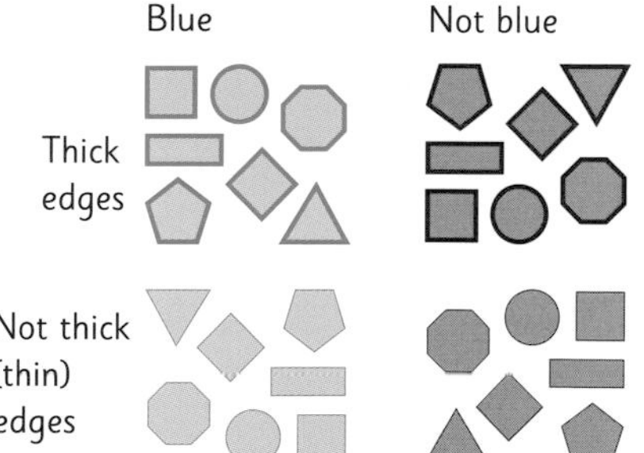

Attributes of colour and thickness.
See **attribute, classification, diagram, group**

space

Space is any 3-D region.

spatial Things that are relating to, or happening in, space. Spatial figures (solids) have three dimensions.

See **dimension, region, solid, three-dimensional**

Examples

a basketball

the Earth

See **three-dimensional**

span

Stretch from side to side, across.

See **handspan**

speed

The rate of time at which something travels; the distance travelled in a unit of time.

Example

A car travelled sixty kilometres in one hour. Its speed was 60 km/h.

See **distance, knot, unit of measurement**

sphere

A 3-D shape like a round ball. It has one curved surface and no corners or edges. Every point on the sphere's surface is the same distance from the sphere's centre.

spinner

A disc used in chance games. It can be spun to produce a random number.

spiral

A curve that goes round and round a central point, getting farther and farther away from it as it goes.

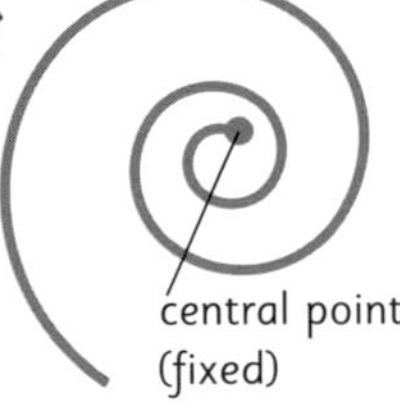

See **curve**

spring balance

An instrument that measures weight or mass. A spring inside the balance is stretched by the force equal to the mass of the object.

See **mass, weight**

square

A quadrilateral with four equal sides and four right angles.

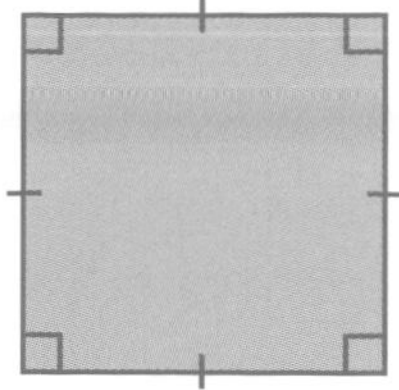

See **quadrilateral, right angle**

square centimetre

Symbol cm^2

A square centimetre is a metric unit for measuring area.

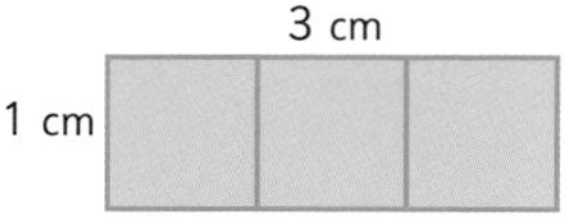

The area of this shape is 3 square centimetres.

$$3 \text{ cm} \times 1 \text{ cm} = 3 \text{ cm}^2$$

See **area, unit of measurement**

square kilometre

Symbol km^2

A metric unit for measuring very large areas, such as part of a country.

$$1 \text{ km}^2 = 1\,000\,000 \text{ m}^2$$

Smaller areas, such as the size of farms, are measured in hectares.

$$1 \text{ km}^2 = 100 \text{ ha}$$

See **area, hecta, unit of measurement**

square metre

Symbol m^2

A metric unit for measuring area.

$$1 \text{ m}^2 = 10\,000 \text{ cm}^2$$

Example

This rug has an area of 4.5 m^2.

See **area, square centimetre, unit of measurement**

square number

A number that can be represented by dots in the shape of a square.

Examples

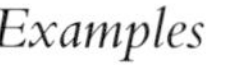

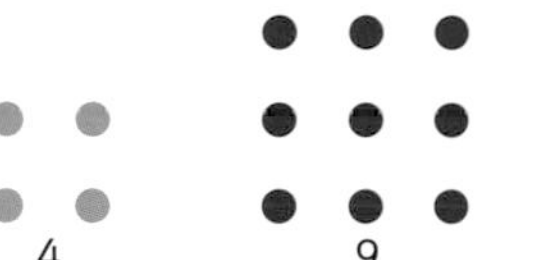

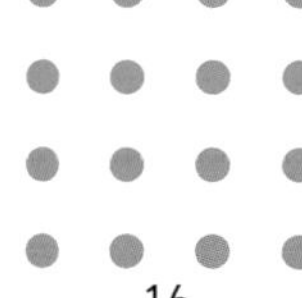

See **rectangular numbers, triangle number**

square of a number

The answer you get when you multiply a number by itself.

$$3^2 = 3 \times 3 = 9$$
$$5^2 = 5 \times 5 = 25$$

$$(0.5)^2 = 0.5 \times 0.5$$
$$= 0.25$$

See **index, square root**

square paper

Paper divided up into squares, which is used for scale drawing and drawing graphs. Square paper is also called graph paper.

Examples

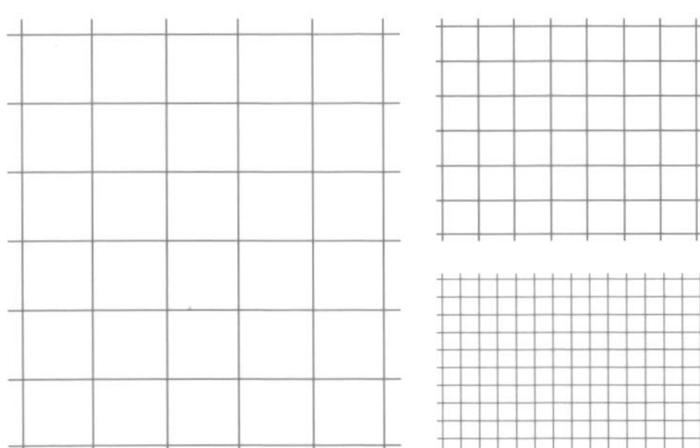

See **dot paper**

square root

A number that, when multiplied by itself, produces the given number. It is the inverse (reverse) of squaring a number.

Square root of 9 (√9) is 3
as 3 × 3 = 9

Square root of 25 (√25) is 5
as 5 × 5 = 25

See **square of a number**

standard unit

Units of measure that are internationally accepted; for example, the metric measures.
See **unit of measurement**

statistics

The collection and grouping of facts in number form. The information collected is called data. Data can be shown in a table or on a graph.

Example

This table shows the favourite foods of a class of 20 children.

Meat	Vegetables	Fruit
Steve P	Rick	Anne
John	Hirani	James
Shi	Trevor	Claire
Tibor	Sam	Ranjit
Jackie		Dean
Sarah		Steve N
David		Belinda
Jeremy		
Darren		

From this data, we can work out percentages.

9 out of 20 children prefer meat:
$\frac{9}{20}$ **= 45%**
of the class prefer meat.

4 out of 20 children prefer vegetables:
$\frac{4}{20}$ **= 20%**
of the class prefer vegetables.

7 out of 20 children prefer fruit:
$\frac{7}{20}$ **= 35%**
of the class prefer fruit.

The percentages are statistics about the food preferences of the class.
See **data, graph, percent**

stone

Symbol st

An imperial unit of weight in the UK.

14 pounds (lb) = 1 stone

See **ounce, pound**

straight angle

An angle of 180°.

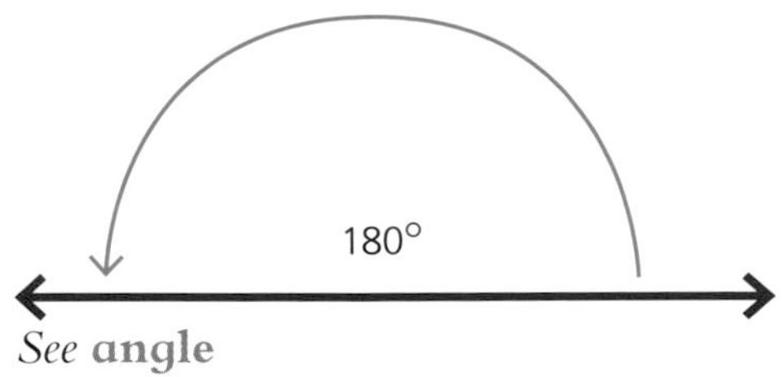

See **angle**

subset

A set within a larger set.

Examples

1. If each element of set S is also an element of set T, then S is called a subset of T.

Set T = {natural numbers to 25}

Set S = {square numbers to 25}

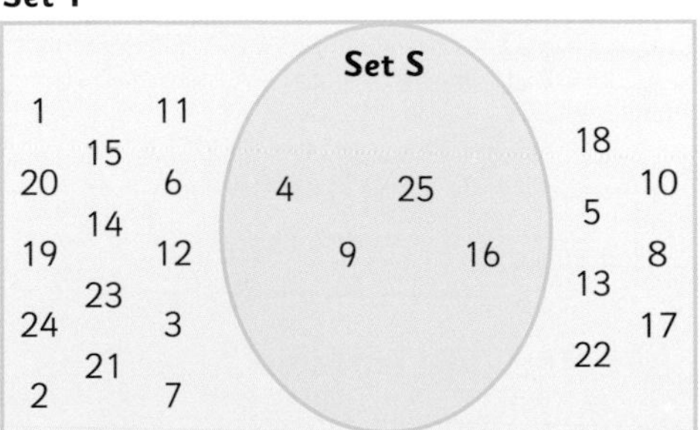

2. Set A = {all children in your class}

Set B = {all girls in your class}

Set B is a subset of set A, because all the elements in set B are also in set A.

See **combination, set**

substitution

1. Something standing in place of another.

Example

If a = 5 and b = 2, what is the value of 2a + 2b?

$$2a + 2b = 2 \times 5 + 2 \times 2$$
$$= 10 + 4$$
$$= 14$$

2. The replacement of a letter in a code message, or a place holder in a number sentence, by a number.

Example

In this secret code, numbers are substituted for letters.

A	B	C	D	E	F	G	H	...
1	2	3	4	5	6	7	8	...

2	1	4	7	5
B	A	D	G	E

See **code, number sentence, place holder**

subtraction

subtract, subtracting

Symbol –

1. Taking away (finding what is left).

Jane had 5 pencils and gave 3 to Jon. How many pencils does Jane have left?

5 – 3 = 2

Jane has 2 pencils.

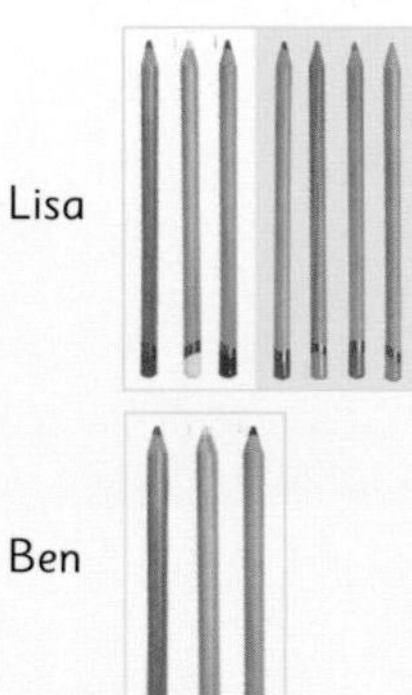

2. Difference (comparison). Lisa has 7 pencils and Ben has 3 pencils. How many more pencils than Ben does Lisa have?

7 – 3 = 4

Lisa has 4 more pencils than Ben.

3. Missing addends (counting on to see how many are missing).

Andy has 3 pencils, but needs 7. How many more must he get?

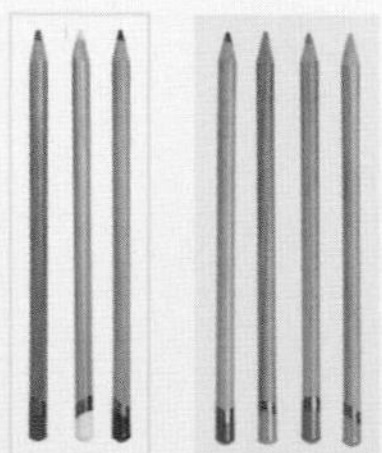

3 + 4 = 7

Andy must get four more pencils.

Subtraction may be represented on a number line.

Example **5 – 3 = 2**

Show on a number line:

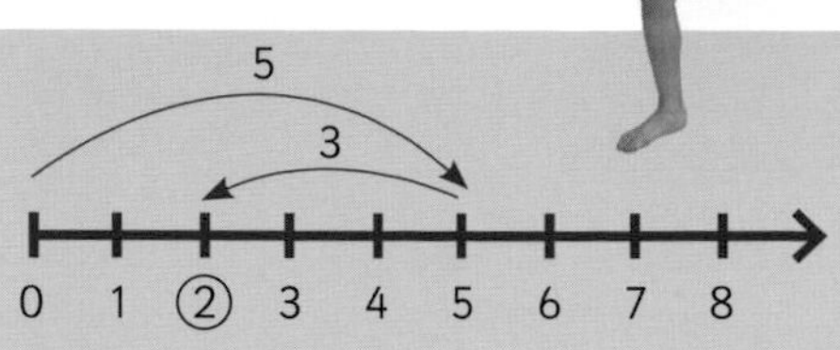

column subtraction Placing the numbers to be subtracted into columns, so that the units, tens, etc, line up. The minuend must be the number at the top and the subtrahend must be the number below.

Example

4 3 5	minuend
– 1 2 3	subtrahend
= 3 1 2	

subtrahend A number that is to be subtracted from another number.

Example

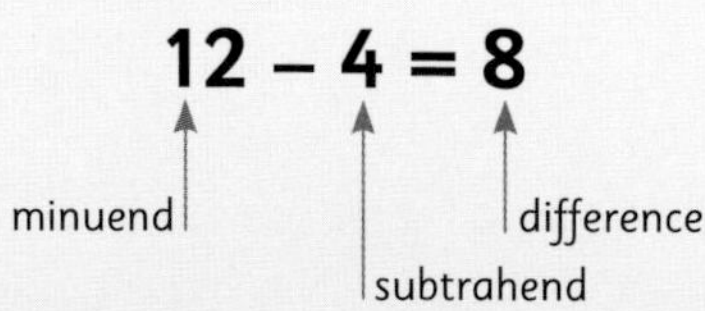

See **difference, minuend, number line**

sum

The answer to an addition problem. It is the total amount when you add together two or more numbers (called addends) or quantities.

Example

3 + 4 = 7

addends: 3, 4 — sum: 7

See **addition**

supplementary angles

Two angles that together make 180°.

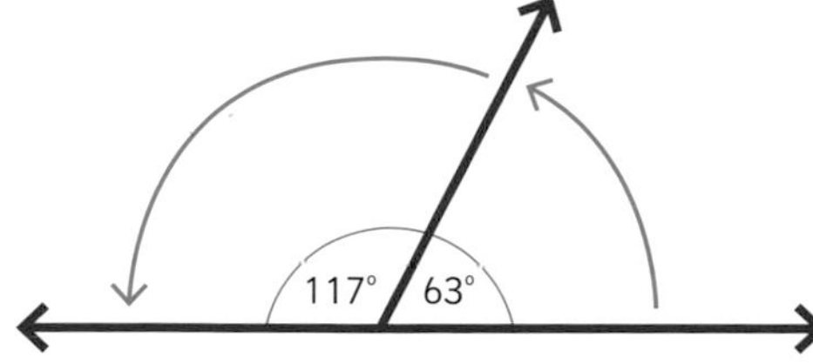

Angles 117° and 63° are supplementary angles.
Angle 117° is called the supplement of 63°.
And angle 63° is called the supplement of 117°.
See **angle, degree**

surface

1. The outside of something.
Example
The surface of the tennis ball is furry.

2. The top level of a liquid.
Example
Plants float on the surface of a lake.

The surface of an object may be flat or curved. *Example*

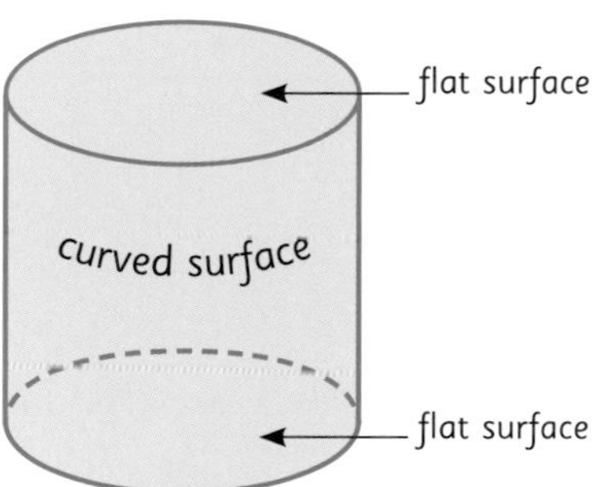

A cylinder has two flat surfaces and one curved surface.

symmetry

A shape has symmetry or is symmetrical when one half of the shape can fit exactly over the other half. Shapes are called symmetrical if they have one or more lines (axes) of symmetry.
See **asymmetry, axis, line of symmetry, rotational symmetry**

Tt

table

1. An arrangement of letters or numbers in rows or columns.

×	1	2	3	4	5	6
1	1	2	3	4	5	6
2	2	4	6	8	10	12
3	3	6	9	12	15	18
4	4	8	12	16	20	24
5	5	10	15	20	25	30
6	6	12	18	24	30	36

2. When multiplication sums are arranged in order, they are called multiplication tables.

Example

The nine times table:

1 × 9 = 9	7 × 9 = 63
2 × 9 = 18	8 × 9 = 72
3 × 9 = 27	9 × 9 = 81
4 × 9 = 36	10 × 9 = 90
5 × 9 = 45	11 × 9 = 99
6 × 9 = 54	12 × 9 = 108

See **multiplication**

take away

remove, subtract

To find the difference between two numbers by removing (subtracting) one number from another. Also called subtraction.

Example

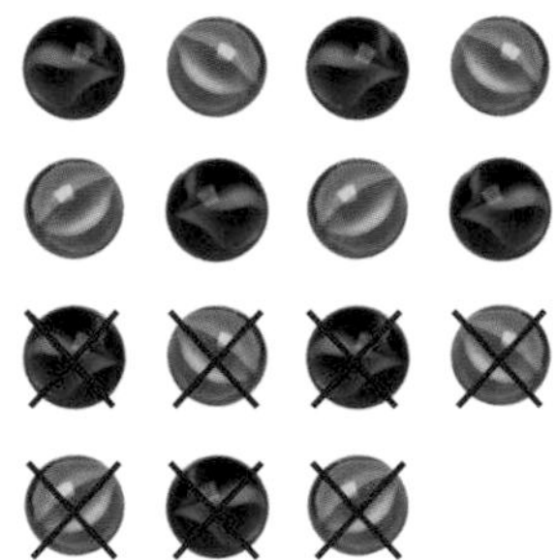

I had 15 marbles, but I lost 7 of them. How many do I have now?

15 – 7 = 8

15 take away 7 leaves eight.
I have 8 marbles left.

See **subtraction**

tally

A way of counting things by making a mark for each item. The marks are usually drawn in groups of five. The fifth mark in each group crosses the other four to make them easy to count.

a tally of 13 items

tangram

A Chinese puzzle made up of a square cut into seven pieces that can be rearranged to make many different shapes.

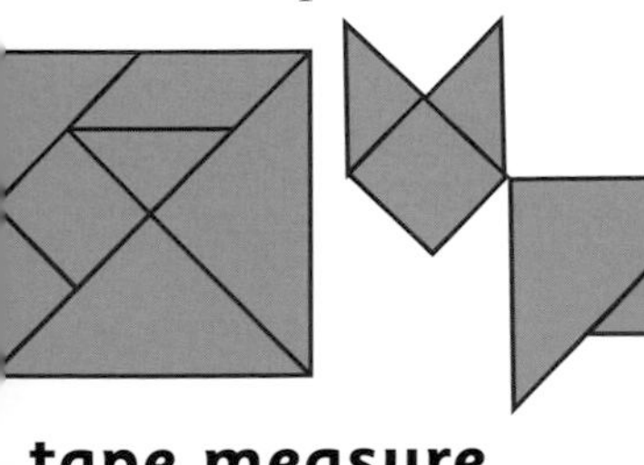

tape measure

A strip of tape or thin metal marked with centimetres.

temperature

How hot or how cold something is. Temperature is measured in degrees Celsius (°C) or degrees Fahrenheit (°F).

1. Water freezes (changes to ice) at 0°C.

2. Water boils (turns to steam) at 100°C.

3. Normal body temperature is about 37°C.

See **Celsius, Fahrenheit, thermometer**

template

A piece of card or plastic for drawing shapes. It may be one of two types:

1. A solid piece of card, plastic, or an object that we draw around.

using a dish as a template

2. A sheet of cardboard or firm plastic out of which shapes have been cut. This is also called a stencil.

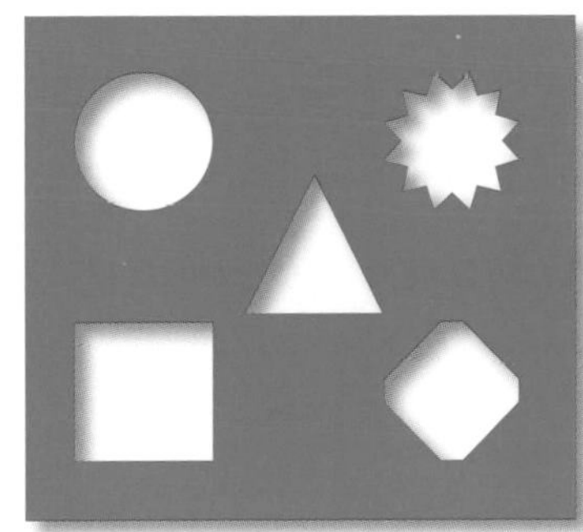

tens

A group of ten things or ten people.

tenth $\frac{1}{10}$

ten thousand Ten groups of a thousand; 10 000.

ten thousandth $\frac{1}{10\,000}$

term

1. Each of the two amounts (quantities) in a ratio or a fraction.

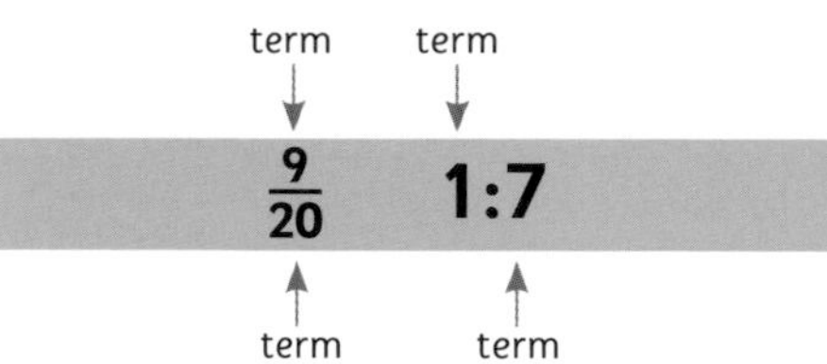

2. Each of the quantities connected by + or – in an algebraic expression or equation.

$$y = x + 1$$

term term

See **algebra, equation**

terminate

To come to an end, finish, to go no further.

terminating decimal

A decimal fraction that is not recurring (continuing). It has an "end".
Example

$$4\overline{)1.00}^{\,0.25}$$

See **decimal, fraction, recurring decimal**

tessellation

tessellate
A group of identical shapes in a repeating pattern, with no overlapping or gaps between them. Regular mosaic and pavement shapes tessellate.

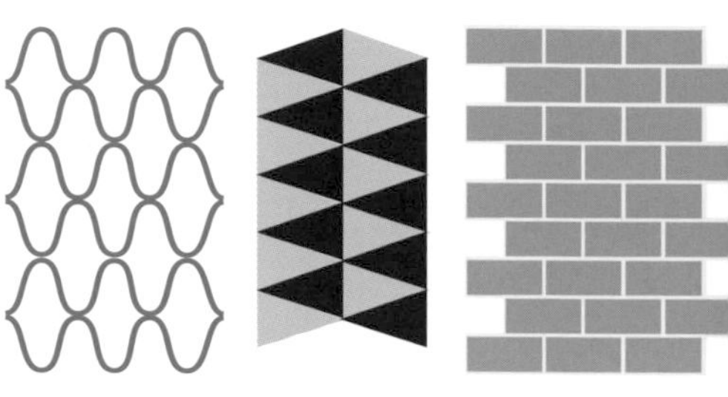

Shapes that can cover a surface completely, like squares, equilateral triangles, and hexagons, are said to tessellate.

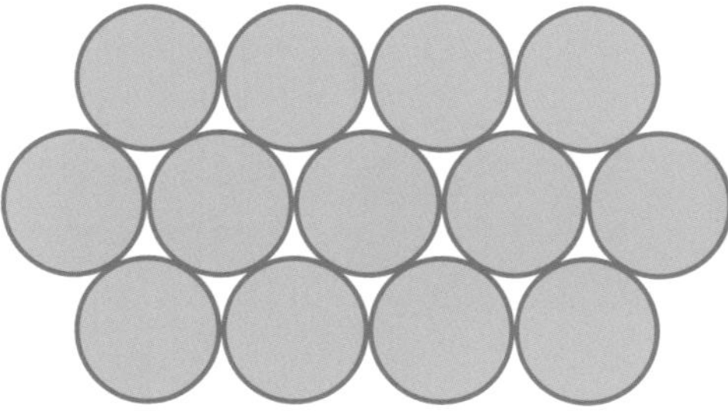

Circles do not tessellate.

See **circle, pattern, plane, square, triangle**

tetragon

A 2-D shape with four sides and four angles.
See **quadrilateral**

tetrahedron

A solid (polyhedron) with four faces. Also called a triangular pyramid. A regular tetrahedron is made of four identical (congruent) equilateral triangles.

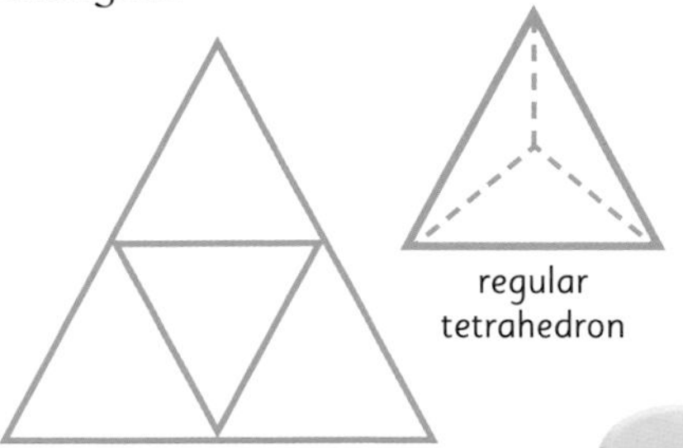

See **polyhedron**

thermometer

An instrument for measuring temperature. This thermometer shows a temperature of 22°C.

See **Celsius, temperature**

third

1. The ordinal number that comes after second and before fourth.

Example He came third in the race.

1st 2nd 3rd 4th

3rd

2. One third means one of three equal parts. Written as $\frac{1}{3}$.

$\frac{1}{3}$	$\frac{1}{3}$	$\frac{1}{3}$

$\frac{1}{3}$ has been coloured in.

See **fraction, ordinal number**

thousand

Ten hundreds, written as 1000.
For numbers longer than four digits, a space is used to divide big numbers into groups of three digits, working backwards from the end.

Example

26375000 is 26 375 000

See **hundred**

three-dimensional

3-D

When something has length, width, and height, it is said to have three dimensions and is called three-dimensional. Solids are three-dimensional.

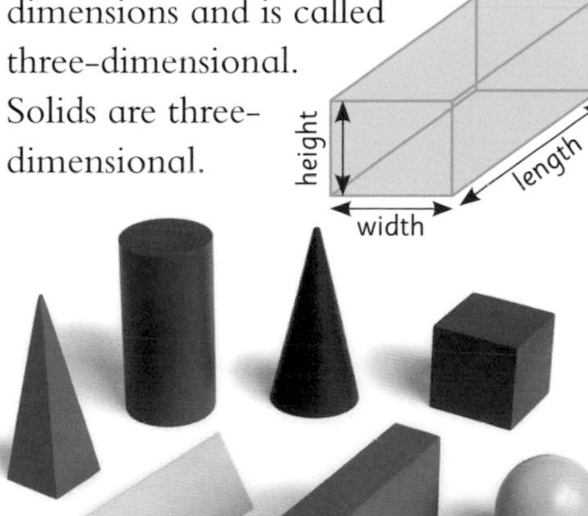

See **dimension, solid, sphere**

time

A way of measuring a particular point in the day or how long something lasts. It helps us measure the past, the present, and the future.

2:00

1 hour = 60 mins

2:15

$\frac{1}{4}$ hour =15 mins

2:30

$\frac{1}{2}$ hour = 30 mins

60 seconds = 1 minute
60 minutes = 1 hour
24 hours = 1 day
7 days = 1 week
52 weeks = 1 year
12 months = 1 year

12-hour time One day divided into two halves of 12 hours each: a.m. is 12 o'clock at night to 12 o'clock in the day, and p.m. is from 12 o'clock in the day to 12 o'clock at night.

a 24-hour clock

24-hour time A period of one day divided into 24 hourly divisions, to prevent errors between a.m. and p.m. times. 8 o'clock at night is 20:00 hours.

a.m. A term used in 12-hour time. It stands for "ante meridiem", which means "before midday".
Example The time is five past five in the morning. It is 5:05 a.m.

p.m. A term used in 12-hour time. It stands for "post meridiem", which means "after midday".

chronological order Events arranged by the date or time when they happened.

decade A period of ten years.

time interval The time that passes between two events.

time line A line on which intervals of time are recorded in chronological order.

1957	1961	1969	1978
Russian dog Laika is first living being to orbit Earth	Yuri Gagarin is first human in space	Neil Armstrong is first man on the Moon	Valentina Tereshkova is first woman in space

times

Another word for "multiplied by".
See **multiplication**

tonne

Symbol t

A tonne is a metric unit for measuring the amount of material that an object contains (mass).
1 t = 1000 kg

The mass of this truck is 1435 kilograms or 1.435 tonnes.
See **kilogram, litre, mass, metric system, weight**

torus

A round 3-D shape with a hole in the middle, like a doughnut or a tire tube.

total

1. Sum. When you add things or values together, the answer is the total.

$$10 + 20 + 25 = \mathbf{55}$$

2. Whole.

See **addition, sum**

transformation

transform

1. Changing the shape, position, or size of an object. This may be done by enlargement, rotation, reflection, or translation.
2. Changing a number or equation to a different form, but with the same result.

$$\frac{1}{2} = 0.5 = 50\%$$

See **enlarge, flip, one-to-one correspondence, projection, reduce, reflection, rotation, translation**

translation

translate

Moving a shape without lifting it, rotating it, or reflecting it.

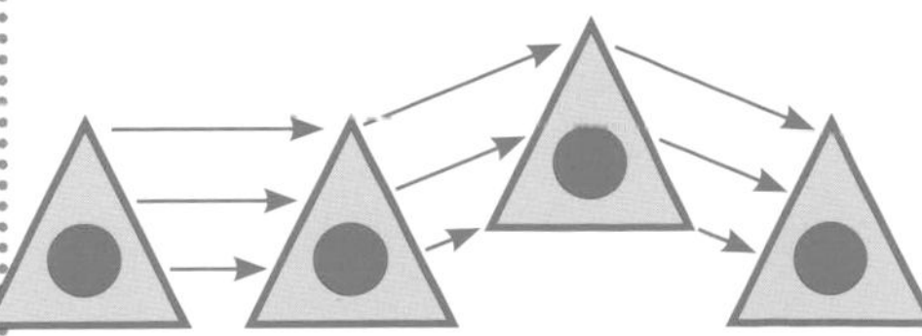

See **flip, reflection, rotation, slide, turn**

trapezium

A four-sided shape (quadrilateral) with one pair of sides parallel and the other pair of sides not parallel.

See **parallel lines, quadrilateral**

trapezoid

A quadrilateral with no parallel sides.

treble

Make three times bigger or multiply by three.

See **multiplication**

tree diagram

A diagram that has a branch-like structure and shows all possible outcomes.

Example

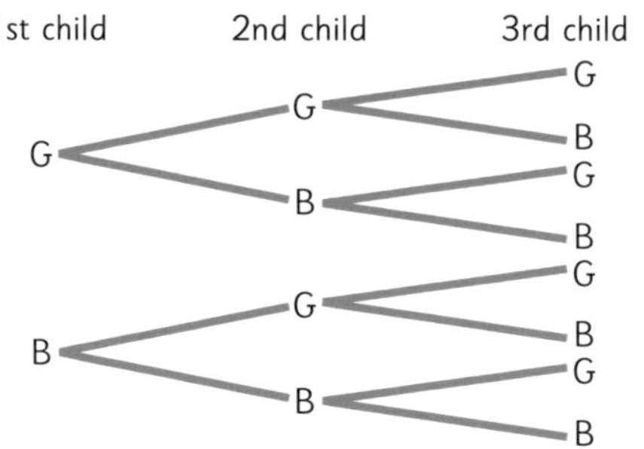

If a family has three children, they may have a boy, then a girl, then a boy; or a girl, then a boy, then a boy, etc. There are 8 possible outcomes.

triangle

A polygon with three sides and three angles. We can classify triangles by sides or by angles. The sum of angles inside a triangle is always 180°.

Examples

1. By sides:

equilateral
(3 sides equal)

isosceles
(2 sides equal)

scalene
(all sides different in length)

2. By angles:

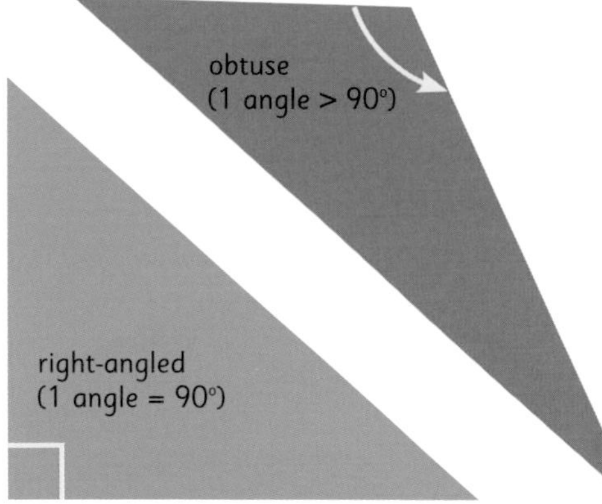

See **equilateral, isosceles triangle, plane, right angle, scalene triangle, sum**

triangle number

triangular number

A number that can be represented by dots in the shape of a triangle.

Examples

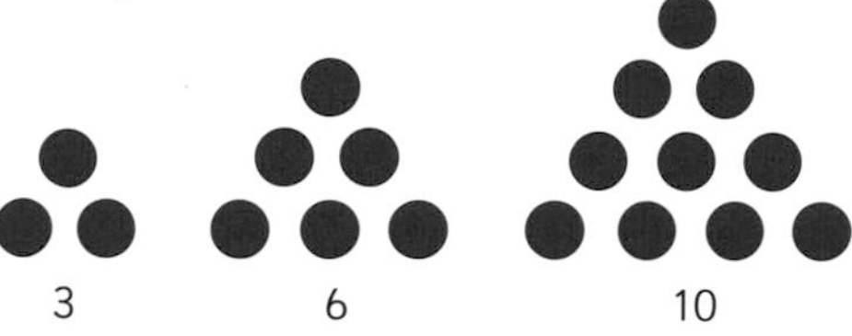

See **triangle**

trillion

A trillion is a million million:

1 000 000 000 000

or 10^{12}

In some European countries, a trillion is a million million million.

true sentence

A sentence about numbers that is true or correct.

Examples

$3 \times 2 = 2 \times 3$ is a true sentence.

$6 \neq 5$ is a true sentence.

The open number sentence

$$2 + x = 9$$

becomes true if x is replaced by 7.

If x is replaced by any other number, then it will become a false sentence.

See **false sentence, number sentence, open number sentence**

turn

To move or change position by rotating.

See **rotation**

twice

Two times, or double.

Example

Twice six is $2 \times 6 = 12$

two-dimensional

2-D

When something has length and width, then it has two dimensions and is two-dimensional. Plane shapes and surfaces have two dimensions.

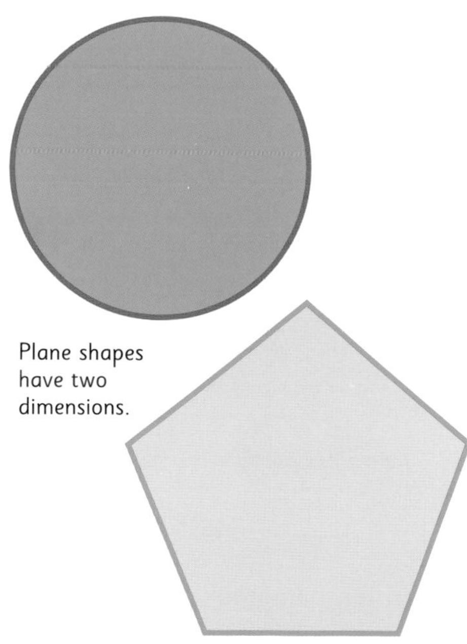

See **dimension, length, plane, region, surface, width**

Uu

unequal

Symbol ≠

Not equal.

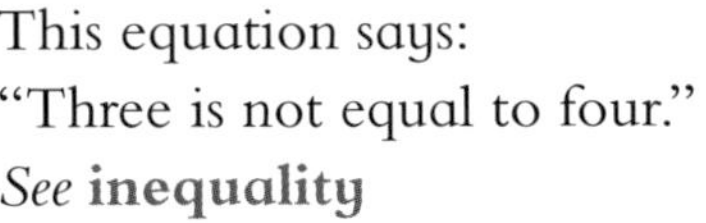

3 ≠ 4

This equation says:
"Three is not equal to four."
See **inequality**

union

A combination of two or more things.

In this Venn diagram, pepper is the union of the sets of vegetables and red objects.
See **set, Venn diagram**

unit

Unit is another name for one.
The unit number is the first number to the left of a decimal point.

In **425.1** the unit is **5**.

↑ decimal point

See **place value, unit of measurement**

unit price

The price at which something is produced or bought.
See **selling price**

unit of measurement

Units we use when measuring things. Standard units are the same sizes across the world.

A **minute** is a unit of time.

The minute hand is pointing to 12.

A **kilometre** is a unit that measures distance.

The Golden Gate Bridge in the USA is 1 kilometre long.

unit square

A square with each side equal to one unit of length or distance.

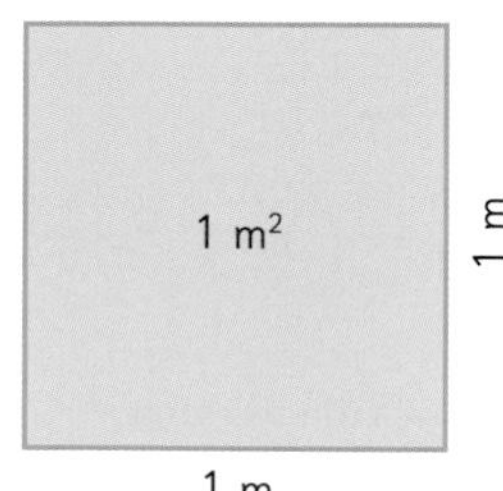

A square with sides one metre long has an area of one square metre (1 m^2).

See **area, distance, length, unit of measurement**

A **gram** is a unit of mass.

500 grams of flour

Other units include litre (to measure volume) and Celsius (temperature).

See **metric system, standard unit**

unknown value

An amount that is not known.

In mathematical sentences, unknown values are represented by variables (symbols or letters).

$$2 \times \square = 10$$

unknown value

$$3a - 2b = 12$$

unknown value

See **variable**

unlike terms

Terms that are not similar. Unlike terms cannot be combined or made simple by adding or subtracting.

2 pineapples + 2 bananas

These fruits are unlike terms, so they cannot be combined to find an answer.

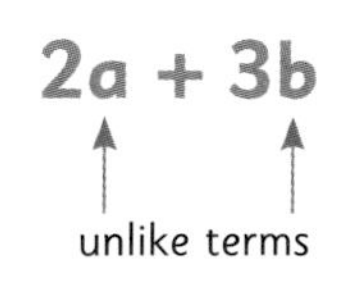

$$2a + a$$

like terms

See **like terms**

a b c d e f g h i j k l m n o p q r s t u v w x y z

value

The value of something is what it is worth.

1. The value of **3 + 5 = 8**.
2. The vase costs $80. Its value is $80.
3. Things of equal value are worth the same. $1 has the same value as 100 cents.

See **evaluate, place value**

vanishing point

The point or points in perspective drawings where all parallel lines appear to meet.

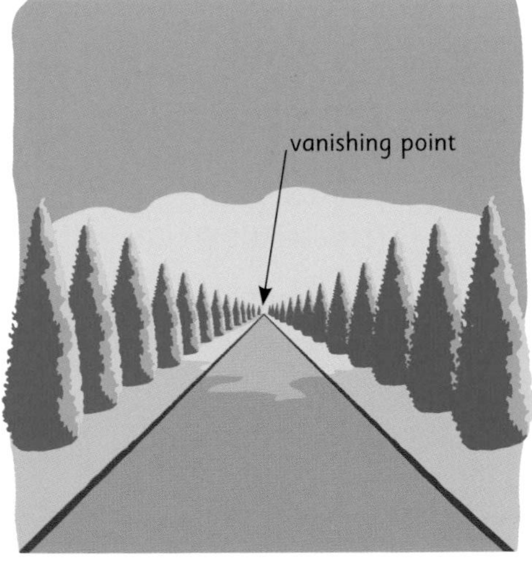

See **perspective**

variable

A symbol or letter that represents an unknown member of a set.

x + 2 = 5

x is the variable

See **constant, number sentence, open number sentence, place holder**

Venn diagram

A Venn diagram is used to sort things into groups or sets. It shows how the sets are related. It is named after Englishman John Venn, who invented it.

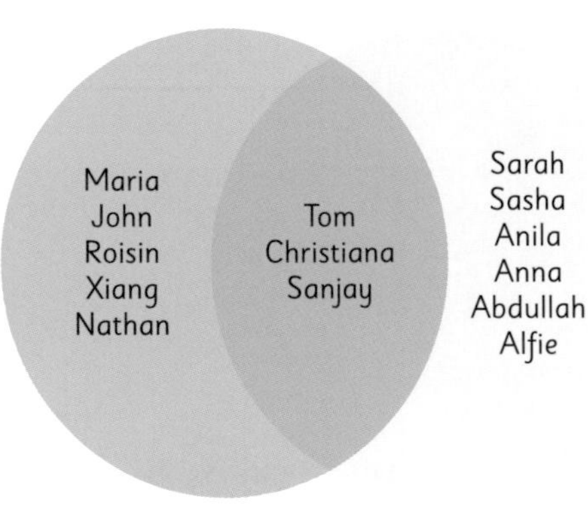

This Venn diagram shows that Tom, Christiana, and Sanjay like both apples and bananas.

See **diagram, set**

vertex

Plural vertices

1. The top; the highest part or point. The vertex is the point opposite the base.
2. A point where two or more adjacent lines meet to form a corner or angle.

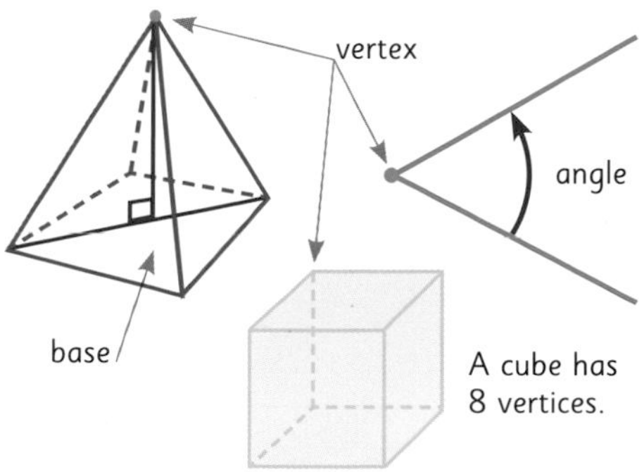

See **adjacent, apex**

vertical

A vertical line is at right angles (perpendicular) to the horizon.

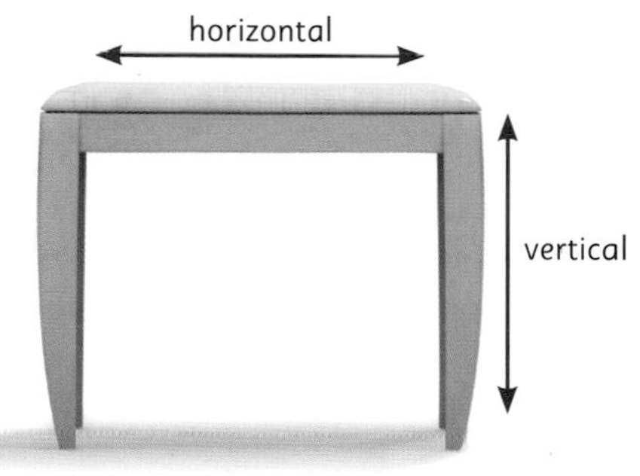

The top of a table is horizontal. The legs of a table are vertical.
See **horizontal line, perpendicular, right angle**

vertically opposite angles

When two lines cross, they make four angles at the point where they meet. The angles opposite each other are equal in size and are called vertically opposite angles.

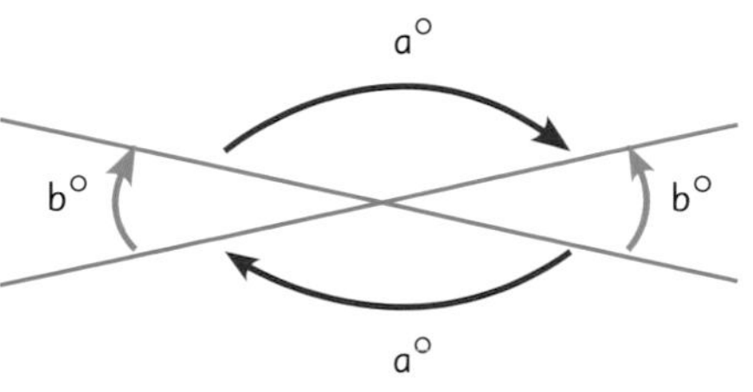

See **angles, parallel lines, vertex**

volume

The amount of space inside a container, or the actual amount of material in the container.

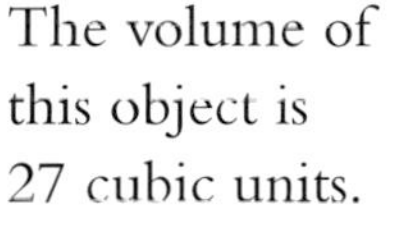

The volume of this object is 27 cubic units.

Some units of volume are:
For solids: cubic centimetre (cm^3), cubic metre (m^3)
For liquids: millilitre (mL), litre (L)
See **capacity, cubic unit**

vulgar fraction

See **improper fraction**

Ww

week
A period of 7 days.

weight
How heavy something is. Weight is the pull of gravity (a force of attraction) on an object. The weight of an object changes if gravitational pull changes, but its mass (the amount of matter it is made of) always remains the same.

Astronauts become weightless in space but the mass of their bodies does not change.

Astronaut on Earth:
His mass = 75 kg
His weight ≈ 75 kg

Astronaut in space:
His mass is still 75 kg
but he is weightless.
People often speak incorrectly of weight when they really mean mass.
See **mass**

whole numbers
Zero together with all counting numbers, but no fractions or decimals.

0 1 2 3 4 5...

See **counting, zero**

width
The measurement of something from side to side. It is also called breadth.

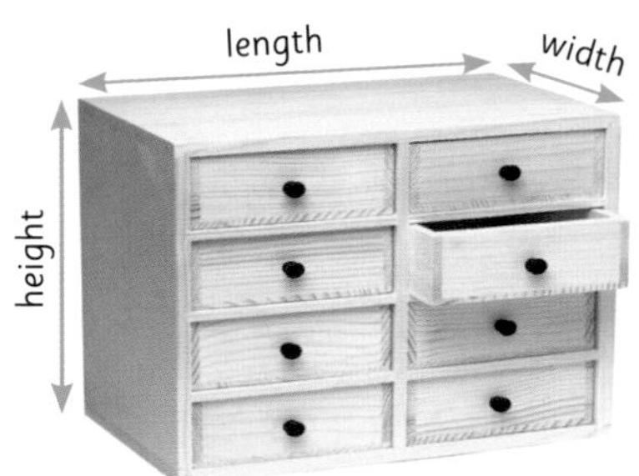

The width of this chest of drawers is 70 cm.

Xx Yy Zz

x-axis, y-axis

See **coordinates**

yard

An imperial measure of length.
1 yard = 36 inches ≈ 91 cm

year

The period of time it takes Earth to make one complete revolution around the Sun: 365 days, 5 hours, and $48\frac{3}{4}$ minutes.
See **time, revolution**

zero

Symbols 0, Ø

The numeral 0 (nought); nothing.
Rules for working with zero:

1. Zero property of addition.
A number + 0 = same number

5 + 0 = 5

2. Zero property of subtraction.
A number – 0 = same number

7 – 0 = 7

3. Zero property of multiplication.
A number × 0 = 0

6 × 0 = 0

4. Zero property of division.
0 ÷ any number = 0

0 ÷ 10 = 0
3 ÷ 0 = can't do

5. A number ÷ 0 has no answer

The digit zero is used as a place holder in numerals.

60

In the number sixty, 0 is a place holder for units. It shows that the 6 means six tens and there are no single units.

These words all mean zero: nil, nought, none, nix, null, oh, void, empty set, zilch, love (in tennis).

See **digit, place holder**

Quick reference

SYMBOLS

symbols	meaning	example
+	add, plus	2 + 1 = 3
-	subtract, take away, minus	7 – 6 = 1
×	multiply by, times	3 × 3 = 9
÷)‾‾‾	divide by	9 ÷ 2 = 4.5
=	is equal to, equal	2 + 2 = 1 + 3
≠	is not equal to	2 ≠ 5
≈ ≑ ≏	is approximately equal to	302 ≈ 300
≤	is less than or equal to	x ≤ 12
≥	is greater than or equal to	y ≥ 6
>	is greater than	7 > 6
<	is less than	2 < 4
≮	is not less than	6 ≮ 5
≯	is not greater than	3.3 ≯ 3.4
¢	cent(s)	50¢
$	dollar(s)	$1.20
p	pence	10p
£	pound	£5.50
€	Euro	€5
.	decimal point (on the line)	5.24
%	percent, out of 100	50%
°	degree (temperature, angle measure)	10°C, 45°F, 90°
’	foot/feet (imperial system)	1’ is approx 30 cm
”	inch/inches (imperial system)	12” = 1’
( ), { }, [ ]	parentheses, brackets	6 + (5 x 2) = 16

^{2}	squared	$3^2 = 9$
^{3}	cubed	$3^3 = 27$
$\sqrt{\ }$	square root	$\sqrt{9} = 3$
π	pi	π is approximately 3.14
∟	right angle, 90°	
⊥	is perpendicular to, at 90°	b h b h
⫽	parallel lines	
\ \\	line segments of the same length	

USEFUL NUMBER WORDS

number	plural	ordinal number
1	ones	first
2	twos	second
3	threes	third
4	fours	fourth
5	fives	fifth
6	sixes	sixth
7	sevens	seventh
8	eights	eighth
9	nines	ninth
10	tens	tenth
100	hundreds	hundredth
1000	thousands	thousandth
10 000	ten thousands	10^4
100 000	hundred thousands	10^5
1 000 000	millions (1,000 thousands)	10^6
1 000 000 000	billions (1,000 millions)	10^9
1 000 000 000 000	trillions (1,000 billions)	10^{12}
1 000 000 000 000 000	quadrillion (million billions)	10^{15}

NUMERICAL PREFIXES

prefix	meaning	example
mono	1	monorail
bi	2	bicycle, binary
tri	3	tricycle, triangle
tetra, quad	4	tetrahedron, quadrilateral
penta, quin	5	pentagon
hexa	6	hexagon
hepta, septi	7	heptagon
octa	8	octagon
nona, non	9	nonagon
deca	10	decagon, decahedron
dodeca	12	dodecagon, dodecahedron
hect	100	hectare
kilo	1000	kilometre, kilogram
mega	1 000 000	megalitre, megabyte
milli	$\frac{1}{1000}$ (one thousandth)	millilitre
centi	$\frac{1}{100}$ (one hundredth)	centimetre

OTHER PREFIXES

prefix	meaning	example
circum	around	circumference
co	together	cointerior, coordinate
counter	opposite, against	counterclockwise
geo	earth	geometry
hemi	half	hemisphere
macro	very big	macrocosmos
micro	very small	microbe
multi	many, much	multilateral
poly	many	polygon
semi	half	semicircle
sub	below, under	subset
trans	across, beyond, over	transverse
uni	one, having one	unit

Units of measurement

LENGTH

metric

10 millimetres (mm)	=	1 centimetre (cm)
100 centimetres (cm)	=	1 metre (m)
1000 millimetres (mm)	=	1 metre (m)
1000 metres (m)	=	1 kilometre (km)

imperial

12 inches (in)	=	1 foot (ft)
3 feet (ft)	=	1 yard (yd)
1,760 yards (yd)	=	1 mile
5280 feet (ft)	=	1 mile
8 furlongs	=	1 mile

AREA

metric

100 square millimetres (mm^2)	=	1 square centimetre (cm^2)
10 000 square centimetres (cm^2)	=	1 square metre (m^2)
10 000 square metres (m^2)	=	1 hectare (ha)
100 hectares (ha)	=	1 square kilometre (km^2)
1 square kilometre (km^2)	=	1 000 000 square metres (m^2)

imperial

144 square inches (sq in)	=	1 square foot (sq ft)
9 square feet (sq ft)	=	1 square yard (sq yd)
1296 square inches (sq in)	=	1 square yard (sq yd)
43 560 square feet (sq ft)	=	1 acre
640 acres	=	1 square mile (sq mile)

MASS

metric

1000 milligrams (mg)	=	1 gram (g)
1000 grams (g)	=	1 kilogram (kg)
1000 kilograms (kg)	=	1 tonne (t)

imperial

16 ounces (oz)	=	1 pound (lb)
112 pounds (lb)	–	1 hundredweight
2240 pounds (lb)	=	1 ton
20 hundredweight	=	1 ton

LIQUID VOLUME

metric

1000 millilitres (mL)	=	1 litre (L)
1 mL (for liquids)	=	1 cm^3 (for solids)
1000 litres (L)	=	1 kilolitre (kL)
1 kL (for liquids)	=	1 m^3 (for solids)

imperial

8 fluid ounces (fl oz)	=	1 cup
20 fluid ounces (fl oz)	=	1 pint (pt)
4 gills (gi)	=	1 pint (pt)
2 pints (pt)	=	1 quart (qt)
4 quarts (qt)	=	1 gallon (gal)
8 pints (pt)	=	1 gallon (gal)

ANGLES

1 right angle	=	90 degrees (90°)
1 straight angle	=	180 degrees (180°)
1 revolution	=	360 degrees (360°)

Conversion tables

LENGTH

metric		imperial
1 millimetre (mm)	=	0.03937 inch (in)
1 centimetre (cm)	=	0.3937 inch (in)
1 metre (m)	=	1.0936 yards (yd)
1 kilometre (km)	=	0.6214 mile

imperial		metric
1 inch (in)	=	2.54 centimetre (cm)
1 foot (ft)	=	0.3048 metre (m)
1 yard (yd)	=	0.9144 metre (m)
1 mile	=	1.6093 kilometre (km)
1 nautical mile	=	1.853 kilometre (km)

AREA

metric		imperial
1 square centimetre (cm^2)	=	0.155 square inch (sq in)
1 square metre (m^2)	=	1.1960 square yard (sq yd)
1 hectare (ha)	=	2.4711 acres
1 square kilometre (km^2)	=	0.3861 square yard (sq yd)

imperial		metric
1 square inch (sq in)	=	6.4516 square centimetre (cm^2)
1 square foot (sq ft)	=	0.0929 square metre (m^2)
1 square yard (sq yd)	=	0.8361 square metre (m^2)
1 acre	=	0.4 hectare (ha)
1 square mile (sq mile)	=	2.59 square kilometre (km^2)

MASS

metric		imperial
1 milligram (mg)	=	0.0154 grain
1 gram (g)	=	0.0353 ounces (oz)
1 kilogram (kg)	=	2.2046 pounds (lb)
1 tonne/metric ton (t)	=	0.9842 imperial ton

imperial		metric
1 ounce (oz)	=	28.35 grams (g)
1 pound (lb)	=	0.4536 kilogram (kg)
1 hundredweight (cwt)	=	50.802 kilogram (kg)
1 imperial ton (t)	=	1.016 tonne/metric ton (t)

VOLUME

metric	imperial
1 cubic centimetre (cm^3)	= 0.0610 in^3
1 dm^3 (decimetre)/1000 cm^3	= 0.0353 ft^3
1 cubic metre (m^3)	= 1.3080 yd^3
1 litre (L)/1 dm^3	= 1.76 pint (pt)
1 hectolitre (hL)/100 L	= 21.99 gallons

imperial	metric
1 cubic inch (in^3)	= 16.387 cm^3
1 ft^3/1,728 in^3	= 0.0283 m^3
1 fluid ounce (fl oz)	= 28.413 mL
1 pint (pt)/20 fl oz	= 0.5683 L
1 gallon/8 pt	= 4.5461 L

TEMPERATURE

To convert from Celsius to Fahrenheit

Times by 9, divide by 5, and add 32 (C x 9) ÷ 5 + 32 = F

To convert from Fahrenheit to Celsius

Minus 32, times by 5, and divide by 9 5 × (Fahrenheit – 32) ÷ 9 = C

HOW TO CONVERT METRIC and IMPERIAL MEASURES

to change	to	multiply by
acre	hectare	0.40
centimetres	feet	0.03
centimetres	inches	0.39
cubic centimetres	cubic inches	0.06
cubic feet	cubic metres	0.03
cubic inches	cubic centimetres	16.38
cubic metres	cubic feet	35.31
feet	centimetres	30.48
feet	metres	0.30
gallons	litres	4.55
grams	ounces	0.04

to change	to	multiply by
hectare	acre	2.47
inches	centimetres	2.54
kilograms	pounds	2.20
kilometres	miles	0.62
kilometres per hour	miles per hour	0.62
litres	gallons	0.22
litres	pints	1.76
metres	feet	3.28
metres	yards	1.09
metres per minute	centimetres per second	1.66
metres per minute	feet per second	0.05
miles	kilometres	1.61
miles per hour	kilometres per hour	1.61
miles per hour	metres per second	0.44
millimetres	inches	0.04
ounces	grams	28.35
pints	litres	0.57
pounds	kilograms	0.45
square centimetres	square inches	0.16
square inches	square centimetres	6.45
square feet	square metres	0.09
square kilometres	square miles	0.38
square metres	square feet	10.76
square metres	square yards	1.19
square miles	square kilometres	2.59
square yards	square metres	0.83
tonnes (metric)	tons (imperial)	0.98
tons (imperial)	tonnes (metric)	1.02
yards	metres	0.91

THE MULTIPLICATION SQUARE (1–12)

×	1	2	3	4	5	6	7	8	9	10	11	12
1	1	2	3	4	5	6	7	8	9	10	11	12
2	2	4	6	8	10	12	14	16	18	20	22	24
3	3	6	9	12	15	18	21	24	27	30	33	36
4	4	8	12	16	20	24	28	32	36	40	44	48
5	5	10	15	20	25	30	35	40	45	50	55	60
6	6	12	18	24	30	36	42	48	54	60	66	72
7	7	14	21	28	35	42	49	56	63	70	77	84
8	8	16	24	32	40	48	56	64	72	80	88	96
9	9	18	27	36	45	54	63	72	81	90	99	108
10	10	20	30	40	50	60	70	80	90	100	110	120
11	11	22	33	44	55	66	77	88	99	110	121	132
12	12	24	36	48	60	72	84	96	108	120	132	144

Acknowledgements

The publisher would like to thank the following for their kind permission to reproduce their photographs:

(Key: a-above; b-below/bottom; c-centre; f-far; l-left; r-right; t-top)

Corbis: John Block / Brand X 55c; Burke / Triolo Productions / Brand X 66tl; Randy Faris 73cl; Joson / Zefa 8cr; Matthias Kulka / Zefa 114-115; MedioImages 36br; Steven Mark Needham / Envision 99fcr; Kelly Redinger / Design Pics 14crb; Thinkstock 47cr; Josh Westrich / Zefa 95crb. **DK Images**: Sarah Ashun 93fcra; Rick and Rachel Bufton 100cl; Jane Bull 1clb, 1crb, 1fbl, 1fbr, 6bc, 34fcl, 38cra, 62crb, 64ca, 104ftr; NASA 118c; Ray Smith 104bl, 104cl, 104cla, 104fcl; South of England Rare Breeds Centre, Ashford, Kent 72cr; Stephen Oliver 2tr, 20bl (cars), 21tr, 43tl, 55cr, 56tl. **Dreamstime.com**: 16tr, 46br (apples), 46br (bananas), 46br (cherries), 46br (oranges), 46br (pears), 91bc, 93fbl, 117bl. **Getty Images**: Allsport Concepts / Nathan Bilow 99cla; De Agostini Picture Library / DEA / C. Dani 101fcra; Image Source 19br, 72bl; Imagenavi / Sozaijiten / Datacraft 80tr; PhotoAlto Agency RF Collections / ZenShui / Laurence Mouton 71ftl, 71tc, 71tl; Photodisc 11bl; Photodisc / Amos Morgan 71br; Photodisc / C Squared Studios 26br, 26crb, 26fbr, 26fcrb; Photodisc / Don Farrall 62cl; Photodisc / Plush Studios 21br; Photodisc / Russell Illig 111bl; Photodisc / SW Productions 107bc; Photographer's Choice / Burazin 61bl; Photographer's Choice / Jose Luis Pelaez Inc 70bl; Photographer's Choice / Kevin Summers Photography 34bl (apples), 34cl (apples); Photographer's Choice / Lew Robertson 26cr, 26cra; PhotosIndia.com 63tl; Riser / David Roth 61fbl; Stockbyte 84tr; StockFood Creative / Gustavo Andrade 66ftl; StockFood Creative / Karl Newedel 86cb; Stone / Gabrielle Revere 59br; Stone / Stuart McClymont 82bl; Stone+ / Diego Uchitel 50cla; Taxi / Space Frontiers / Dera 100ftr; Westend61 / Creativ Studio Heinemann 45cr. **iStockphoto.com**: 45RPM 76br; bbszabi 49clb; Graham Klotz 61cr.

All other images © **Dorling Kindersley**
For further information see: **www.dkimages.com**